Bouncing Back
Surviving (and thriving) between jobs

Jennifer B. Anderton

Copyright © 2013 Jennifer B. Anderton

All rights reserved.

ISBN:1493775707
ISBN-13:9781493775705

DEDICATION

This book is dedicated to everyone who found that losing their job was not the end, but the beginning.

CONTENTS

	Acknowledgments	i
1	Why Losing Your Job Could Be the Best Thing to Happen	3
2	Making Peace With the Past	15
3	I Was What?	21
4	Unemployment: The Long Wait	25
5	Many Paths	32
6	Organizing Your Job Hunt to Maintain Your Sanity	36
7	New Beginnings: Getting in the "Hire Me" Mindset	43
8	Ethics, Loyalty, Manners and Other Little Things	53
9	Sites to Know, Sites to Ignore	62
10	By the Numbers	76
11	The Job Hunting Year	80
12	The Emotional Rollercoaster	84
13	Dealing With Rejection	89
14	Going Back	92
15	I Was…	96
16	Mission Accomplished	100

ACKNOWLEDGMENTS

Thanks go to my fiancé Blake who told me that I was wonderful before a job and I was still wonderful after it. Thanks also go to my parents Richard and Bonnie who showed me that who you are to those you love matters more than who you are on a piece of paper.

1
WHY LOSING YOUR JOB COULD BE THE BEST THING TO HAPPEN

Maybe the signs have been there for months, a gradual vacancy of offices and cubicles. On the other hand maybe the writing's been on the wall "Danger! The end is near!" flashing before your eyes. Or you might be like millions of workers toiling away on a Friday afternoon, doing your job when your boss calls, "Come to my office. We need to talk." It's then your stomach crashes to the floor because somehow you sense this isn't a talk it's The Talk.

It's Friday afternoon and you are now unemployed.

You may be the only one in your company let go that day, or you may be one among thousands clutching your pink slip, no matter what you're not alone. At any given time there are millions of people between jobs.

This book is designed to help you get back on your feet. Losing your job can shake you to your core and destroy your self-confidence. "If they don't want me nobody else will" you say. Bouncing Back is about gaining perspective, learning from the experience, and becoming a stronger more confident future employee.

You Are Not Alone: Famous Firings

Although you may feel like you are the only person to have ever been fired, you're not. You may also be saying to yourself, "Now that I've been fired that's it. I'll never amount to anything." Nothing could be further from the truth. So many famous and influential people got their start only after they were fired the case could be argued that failing is a prerequisite for success.

In 1919, an editor at the Kansas City Star fired an employee citing the employee "lacked imagination and had no good ideas". Undeterred the employee bought an animation studio, Laugh-O-Gram which he drove into bankruptcy. If this man had given up the world would never have known Mickey Mouse, Imagineering, or all of the other things that sprang from his, Walt Disney's imagination. If he hadn't been fired for being unimaginative no one would have seen his creative talent.

One of the richest and most powerful women of the modern world got her start by losing her job as a news reporter and accepting a consolation job on local daytime television. It was there hosting 'People Are Talking' that Oprah Winfrey found her niche and turned it into a media empire allowing her to pay it forward with programs inspiring women and girls around the globe.

1989 was a year that saw layoffs affecting employee's at all corporate levels. Handy Dan was a home-improvement chain with two employees, Bernie Marcus and Arthur Black. Both men were among many employees fired when Handy Dan was raided by another corporation. Marcus and Black decided this was the ideal opportunity to launch a business idea they'd had while working at Handy Dan's. Home Depot was born, quickly growing to become one of the largest and most profitable home improvement stores in the United States.

Being CEO does not make you immune to being fired. Instead the case can be made that as a CEO you walk around with a large target on your back quickly blamed for everything that goes wrong.

Being at the top also doesn't mean that you're immune to personality clashes. Lee Iaccoca knew this all too well after rising to the top of Ford Motor Company. He had numerous disagreements with Henry Ford Jr. at that time the CEO and chairman. Finally Iacocca was let go. He soon found himself free to join Chrysler. It was a sinking ship teetering on the verge of bankruptcy, but Iacocca saw opportunity. Iacocca served as CEO of Chrysler until 1992, not only saving the company from failure but introducing management and leadership styles that are studied in business schools today.

Although only four examples are listed here nearly everyone who is admired as a "success", today was at one time labeled as a failure at a job and fired. Indeed it can be said that to be a success it's best to have failed at least once. Anna Wintour the editor of Vogue tells her fashion students "I recommend you all get fired".

Signs You're On the Way… Out That Is

Firings and layoffs rarely come completely out of the blue. Through you may be caught completely off guard chances are if you stop to think about it signs were there. Some of these signs include:

1. Mysterious Meetings: Have you always been part of a team only to find that now they're having meetings without you? If you're feeling bold, ask. An evasive answer with averted eyes says a lot.
2. Social Isolation: When coworkers sense or know that you're on the way out they may stop dropping by your office to chat and you're invitations to lunch, coffee, or drinks may be met with vague and evasive answers.
3. Did You Do Something Wrong: This is not the kind of wrong like misspelling your boss's name on a memo (though people have been fired for less). This type of mistake is losing large amounts of money, breaking the law, placing the company in a compromising position, or breaking the morals clause of your company (if they have one).
4. Corporate Problems: If the company you work for is

sinking fast or hemorrhaging money your job is on shaky ground. If your company is being investigated by any law enforcement or regulatory agencies be careful. Even if you had no knowledge of whatever is being investigated there is still a chance you'll get fired because of guilt by association (no matter how tenuous that association). You should also be wary if your company was recently bought, sold, or otherwise part of a merger. Cleaning house is common in such cases.

5. Do You Have One of "Those" Jobs: One way to find out is to see how many people have had the job before you, how long have they stayed, and why did they leave? If you are the sixth employee in two years and all your predecessors were let go for vague reasons, you might be in an impossible job. Another sign is a deliberate and persistent vagueness about what your duties are and who you report to. An impossible job is one doomed to fail from the start and is more a result of failure to clearly define the scope of the job rather than a failure on the employee's part.

6. Have Other Employees Given You Hints: Cryptic phrases such as "it's always the little ones/new ones they like to fire" are coworkers trying to give you hints.

7. Has Your Environment Changed: Do you now have a smaller office? Have your perks changed?

8. Is Your Job Being Advertised: Your company might want to get a jump start on replacing you. It's really cruel and unkind, but that's business for you.

9. The Popularity Contest: Doing great work is one thing, but if all your coworkers hate you (seeing a dart board with your picture on it is not a good sign); you know who'll be voted off the island first.

10. The Absent Boss: You used to just walk down the hall and talk to your boss, but now they seem to hide behind email. It's good to document everything, but if this is taken to an

extreme it can mean that your boss is laying the foundation for firing you. They're not worried about covering your ass; they're worried about covering their ass from any potential lawsuit. In addition your boss may not want to face you knowing that they will soon be firing you.

11. Has Your Work Changed: Being given vague fluffy projects could mean that you're in the departure lounge. You're being given busy work while they figure out how to get rid of you. If you have one of those impossible jobs this usually won't work since a characteristic of impossible jobs is their amorphous and vague nature.
12. How Much Time Have You Spent In Class: This is a tricky one, as you have to consider if you're being trained on new things (software, policy, etc.), or are they retraining you on things? If it's the latter than they may be trying to cover their asses. You're on the way out and if it ever comes up they'll be able to point out all the effort they went to trying to help you.
13. Its Friday: Studies have consistently shown that Friday is the preferred day to give employees the bad news. There are several theories about why, but I've never heard an employee say "Thank goodness I was laid off on Friday, Wednesday would have been so much worse!" Getting paid off is awful no matter the day.

The Talk

If you're the recipient of a personal chat, chances are the person firing you (it may not be your manger, it just has to be anyone given the authority to do so) will call you into their office, a conference room, any empty room. Your office is your center of power where you're behind the desk. An essential part of being fired is being stripped of your power (even if it is only over the coffeemaker), so everything will be done to fire you either in a neutral location, or one where the person firing you has the power. In addition in your office you might have weapons or things that could be used as weapons while you know you wouldn't do anything rash (hopefully) the person firing you won't want to take that chance. Now some clever person reading this will think, "As long as I don't leave my office they can't fire me." Wishful thinking. Doing that may result in police being called and you being forcefully ejected from the building. Not a good final impression to make.

So suck it up and go to the room.

How To Behave

Almost all firings follow a standard script. The person doing the firing will introduce themselves (if you didn't already know them) and will use some tactic to verify who you are (it's not good to fire James Jones when you meant to fire Jones James). This is not the time to play secret agent and make them guess. As much as you might hate this person right now, you need to try and not piss them off. They might be an ally later on.

Introductions finished the next thing you're likely to hear is "This is very hard for me to do." It may actually be very hard for them to do, they may be saying it because some handbook told them it sounded empathetic, or for some reason they may actually like firing people, but none of that matters. Your only job while the initial firing process is taking place is to sit there, remain calm, do whatever you can to not cry, and try to absorb as much of what is being said as possible. Try not to take it personally. It's just business to your employer. Oh, don't forget to breathe. Passing out is dramatic but ultimately only serves to lengthen the process.

What to Say/What Not to Say

You've survived the firing monologue, now what? It's time for your say and at this point what you say (and how you say it) is just as (if not more) important than what you do not say.

What to Say:
- Ask why you are being fired. Try to get as specific an answer as

possible. Understand that the person firing you may be prohibited from telling you or they may not know. Still try.
- Ask what your former coworkers are being told about your leaving. This is important because the company rumor mill could seriously damage your reputation.
- Thank the person firing you for the opportunity to work for them. You don't have to go overboard with the praise. If all you can manage is a simple 'thank you' that's better than nothing. At this time it will seem very surreal and pointless, but it's important for future contact.
- Ask about your severance. If it is available to you than make sure to negotiate for the best package possible. Don't sign the agreement until you're sure it's what's been agreed upon.
- Ask for a reference. This is perhaps the hardest thing to do. It also requires you to gauge the likelihood of getting one. If you're being fired because you stole from the company I'd skip this step because you're not going to get one. If you get along well with your boss and you're being laid off because the company is going bankrupt, you stand a better chance of getting a reference. The important thing to remember is that a reference is almost never offered, it's something you have to ask for. (Note: You ask for a reference, begging for one doesn't look good. How good do you think a reference you begged for would be anyway?)

What Not to Say:
- Anything that could ever be construed as a threat in any way. This goes for threats against the company, its employees, anything. Do not even attempt to make a joke about it, guaranteed the humor will be lost as the police are called.
- Do not threaten, joke, and insinuate that you will kill or hurt yourself. It will not get your job back but it might earn you a reputation as the crazy person that was fired and a trip to the psych ward.
- Resist every urge to let loose with what you really feel about your

boss, coworkers, and company. No matter how deserved it is, if you do this then you are eliminating potential references.
- Do not beg for your job back. This almost never works. Once they've made up their mind to fire you that's it.

Chances are this conversation will be over in a few minutes, but once it's over try to relax. Getting fired is one of the greatest fears people have. You've just survived it. You're still breathing. Just a few more things to do, but for now know that you faced your fear and walked away stronger for it.

Saying Goodbye to Coworkers

Often coworkers will make themselves scarce right before someone is fired only to reappear afterward. Be nice to your coworkers, chances are they had no say in your firing. In addition make sure to exchange (personal not work) contact information. Your coworkers can act as strong references so make sure to stay in contact with them. Whatever you do don't badmouth or say anything you'll regret about your now former employer or the people who work there.

Cleaning Out

One of the last things you'll do is clean out your workspace be it a locker, cubical, or office. What makes this even more nerve wracking is that in all likelihood the person who just fired you will be there breathing down your neck making sure that every paperclip is accounted for.

A good rule of thumb is to not bring anything into the office that you don't mind leaving at the office…forever. Make copies of the photos on your desk and if it's sentimental leave it at home. If you can see your firing coming try to take personal items home in advance.

You want to clear out your workspace as quickly as possible and with a minimum number of trips to your vehicle. Try to snag boxes from the copy room for this purpose. Methodically go through your desk, open every drawer making sure to take your belongings and only your belongings. Resist the urge to take company property; chances are you'll be caught. For this reason do not destroy or damage company property.

If you have a computer make sure to remove all your personal files. In addition if you have any personal emails send them to your personal account or delete them. Do not install viruses or malicious software. This is a no-brainer that you will be caught.

Now that personal items have been taken all that remains is the work product, in one word, no. That awesome proposal you worked on, that great training presentation you gave. If you worked on it for your company or on company time, it's considered property of your company. It belongs to them and if you take it you are subject to persecution for all sorts of nasty things such as theft of company property.

In Writing

Same general guidelines except that you don't have to smile politely during the process. The drawback is that any opportunity to ask for a reason why or for a reference is lost. Being fired is often referred to as "getting the pink slip". Truth is no one knows exactly where the term comes from and in other countries the firing slip comes in different colors. Still no matter what color a firing letter comes printed on it's still a firing letter.

The Aftermath

You made it out of the office. Hopefully you remembered all your stuff, to turn in your badges and keys, and sign all your paperwork because the last thing you want to do is go back in there.

If you drove to work, make it to your car and lock the doors. Cry your heart out. Scream out all your rage, hurt, and frustration. Pound the steering wheel. It's best not to do this in a convertible with the top down. This is your time; you kept it together now let it out. Doing this is extremely important not only for your emotional well-being (it's not healthy to keep these emotions in), but it's very dangerous to drive in such an emotional state. Getting in an accident or getting a ticket makes an already awful day infinitely worse. So cry it out, wipe your eyes, take a few deep breaths to compose yourself and then, and only then, think about driving.

If you commute you have a few options. You can make it home before you breakdown. You can find some place (like a park) nearby and cry. A potential hazard is running into a now former coworker. Or you can call a friend for a ride. True you'll end up explaining what happened, but you may end up with a friendly shoulder to cry on.

If you carpool then either you arrange other transportation, or have the most awkward drive home you have ever had.

The Days Following

The days after you've been fired are likely to be a rollercoaster of emotions. One moment hopeful and positive the next depressed and despondent. No matter your emotional state there are certain things that you should and should not do.

Things You Should Do:
- Get over being ashamed. You are not the only person who has ever been fired. If it makes you question your self-worth just look at successful people, many of them were fired at one point. Think of it as a rite of passage if it makes you feel better, but don't be ashamed.
- Sort out your finances. You need to have an accurate picture of where you stand financially. Doing this will help you plan your between-job expenses. If you're scared to do this remember that knowledge is power and you don't have to show this to anyone if you don't want to.
- Unemployment. If you're eligible for it file sooner rather later as claims offices often have a processing backlog. It can be weeks between when you file a claim and when you receive

your first check. In addition if you're asked for an interview to gather more information this adds weeks to the process. As for the stigma of unemployment remember that a portion of your paycheck when you were working paid into the unemployment fund.
- Do you have health insurance? If you do find out how long it's effective. Schedule any doctor's appointments to take advantage of your health insurance benefits while you still have them.
- Reach out to coworkers. Hopefully you exchanged contact information. Now is the time to drop a message, arrange coffee dates. Be prepared to answer questions about how and why you left, but remember to be professional. Ultimately you're there for a reference not to dish gossip or complain.
- Analysis and reflection. It is important to objectively look at what you do well and what went wrong about your former job. This process is done throughout this book. The tendency is to either see only the positive or only the negative, the key is to find balance because that's where growth comes from.

Things You Should Not Do:
- Dish about your former employer on social media sites. Future employers may read this and think "If they said this about them, will they say the same about us". So how do you vent (and to who)? Some career specialists will say no one, but you have to vent. Just be very careful to whom you vent and where you vent (You never know who is standing behind you in line at the grocery store).
- Anything that breaks the law. An arrest record of any sort will make getting a new job infinitely harder, not to mention court fees will drain your savings.
- Bury your head in the sand. While this is an attractive option the longer you bury your head in the sand the longer it will take

you to make meaningful plans and move forward. You're stuck at a time you need to be making some key decisions. Strike a balance between downtime and planning time, what that balance is you have to decide.

2
MAKING PEACE WITH THE PAST

The problem with the past is that it's always right there behind you, the good and the bad, just over your shoulder haunting you. No matter what you do your past follows you. When you've lost your job and are looking for a new one your past can be your worst enemy sabotaging you and holding you back from being able to move forward. Before you jump back into the job hunting scene it is imperative that you make peace with the past and what happened at previous jobs.

What happens if you don't do this? The frustration, negativity and anger over what happened will express itself making it more difficult to approach job hunting with a clear mind (you'll find yourself thinking "why bother? Every other company will screw me over just like the last one") and that negativity will express itself on your applications making it harder to get interviews. If you do land an interview this negativity will be readily apparent. At the worst it will lead you to make comments and behave in such a way as to make interviewers think you're a loose cannon of resentment and hostility. At the best you'll be able to hide your negative thoughts and feelings but in doing so you'll be distracted and have difficulty answering the questions. Now your interviewer just thinks you're unfocused and you don't really care about the interview or the job.

Who are you?

In the working world people are most identified by what they do, their job and title. It's almost automatic "Hi I'm Jane and I'm an architect" or "I'm Peter a chef". This becomes even more pronounced with professional degrees. Suddenly you're "Dr. Sarah" or "Professor Michael" everywhere you go. What's the problem? I worked hard for those titles and clarifications. Why shouldn't I use them? On many levels nothing is wrong. The problem becomes if this becomes your only identity.

If you primarily identify yourself by your occupation, title, or job, what happens when you lose your job? Who are you then?

There is one essential point to take away from this chapter: **you are more than whatever job you have**. The sooner you realize this the easier it will be to move on from losing your job and focus on finding a new one.

There are some obvious signs that you are over-identified with your job. When you do have a job is that all you talk about? It's one thing to talk about work at work, or while at work functions, but what about at home? Is it the only thing you talk about with your spouse, partners, and friends? Do you relate every topic of conversation to something, someone, or a situation at work? If you can't think of the last time you had a conversation without referring to work chances are you're too invested in work. Worried that your invested in work to the extreme? The worst cases I've run across are partners who will stop during the middle of sex to write down an idea for a problem at work they were thinking about.

What about between jobs? Since you don't have a job you can't have a work identity to become immersed in, right? Wrong. The job hunter identity can be even more consuming. You tell everyone who will listen, especially those closest to you of every up and down in your job hunt. You dissect every opportunity. When you feel yourself ready to go insane, imagine how your partner and friends feel as the captive audience to your endless job-hunting monologue.

Developing an identity outside of work will also make you a more attractive potential employee. It gives you something to connect with interviewers about. Interviewers see so many people that something that sets you apart from the crowd and helps to make you memorable (in a good way) is always helpful. In addition while you are being hired as an employee, you are also a person, employers (usually) like to hire people (except for the occasionally oddball company).

Entire sections of bookstores are devoted to various hobbies and interests, and the purpose of this book is not to spend reams of paper telling you what other books can. What is important is that you do whatever you can to create a work-life balance. Doing so will not only make you a better employee, but will also make it easier to cope with the time between jobs.

Making the Best of the Situation

One of the first things newly let go employees think is, "I must have been fired because of my performance". In reality even if you're explicitly told you're being let go because of your performance, which may not be the case. "Poor performance" is the generic catch all "etc." of Human Resources. This is especially true in the case of the impossible job and if upon being let go you ask for a more specific answer and are denied one (bonus points if the person you ask stammers, averts their gaze, and otherwise grows very nervous).

That being said there are things you should do and have to do in order to not only survive, but also thrive (after all survival is good but thriving is better).

1. Talk to Human Resources: Do this before you leave (ideally). Why? They're the ones who will be able to answer your questions. Think you were fired illegally? Ask them. If you think that they already know so it's not worth asking, wrong. They may have no idea, the person letting you go may have

forgotten (or purposely not told) Human Resources. In addition Human Resources will be the place you contact for information about all your after-employment benefits (severance, health, insurance, etc.).

2. Family and Friends: At this time the support of your family and friends is essential. They'll be the ones to hold you while you cry, help make you laugh, and provide a sounding board for your ideas. That is great, but in one respect resist asking for their support... borrowing money. An old adage holds true 'the quickest way to lose friends is to borrow money from them'. Borrowing money from family and friends instantly changes the dynamics of the relationship. Not only will you have the added stress of having to pay back the money, but your financial life will be an open book. Did a friend loan you money for groceries? Then you'll find yourself asking 'Does this mean I can only buy the bare minimum? Can I buy coffee or is that an extravagant expense?' and other questions. If this sounds like a lot of stress and hassle that's only for borrowing a few dollars from a friend. Add the emotional entanglements of family relationships to the mix and it's virtually guaranteed to end in fights and hurt feelings.

3. Another Thing to Avoid: Quick loan companies. While you will be avoiding the emotional minefield of borrowing from family and friends you'll also be incurring a very large debt that at the moment you have absolutely no way of paying back. It's easy to borrow and impossible to pay back.

4. Spreading the News: Honesty is essential, the gory details are optional. Be honest and calmly lay out a plan. Even if you keep separate finances it's important to communicate so that you and your partner are on the same page. What about children? Approach the subject in an age-appropriate manner. Children can sense stress and will blame themselves in absence of knowledge and information. View this as a chance to teach your children valuable life skills. Talk about the need to be

thrifty and resourceful. Be an example of how to handle stress and bounce back from disappointment. Show your children that just because bad things happen that does not make them a bad person. Remove the shame about losing you job. Chances are your children will have similar experiences in their life. How you act now will serve as a model for them.

5. Owing the Event: Step back and honestly assess what role you might have played in losing your job. Were you chronically late? Own up to it. If you don't learn from your mistakes than you're doomed to repeat them. But how do you prevent owning your mistakes from turning into a depressing pity party? One way is to list the top five (or first) five on a piece of paper with space in-between each number. Write these as one sentence statements being as concrete as possible. An alternative is to get five index cards and write the statements on one side of each card. In any case once you have your statements use the space in-between to write how you can change or prevent this from happening in the future. In addition write one sentence about how you would respond if an interviewer questioned you about this. Remember to be proactive and positive. An example of this is:

   A. Issue: Chronically late for work.
   B. Solution: Set multiple alarm clocks. Allow extra time.
   C. Statement: I have learned how important it is to be on time and be a person my co-workers can depend on. This was an opportunity to learn and grow.

Thinking of a problem does no good unless you think of the solution.

6. Process the Emotions: In the days following your job loss your emotions will be all over the place. At one moment you'll be crying convinced the world has ended. The next moment you'll be excited about all the new possibilities. Throw in anger, fear, resentment and a thousand other bouncing emotions. So how do you handle it all and keep

your sanity? Don't stuff it down or try to ignore it. Find ways to express your feelings. Writing, painting, dancing, long walks, boxing, anything to help you process your emotions. Once you work through them you'll be able to move forward with a clear head. What to avoid? Burying your emotions with drugs and alcohol. They may temporarily numb your pain, but eventually you'll have to deal with your emotions in order to move forward. In addition a DUI or drug conviction will be a lot worse on a job application than losing your job.

7. Self-Care: You are going through a stressful time, but how you take care of yourself will help to determine how effective you are. Exercise, even if it's just walking around the block will provide fresh air and a chance to clear your head. In addition eating healthy will help to add much needed stability to your routine. Finally a common thought among job hunters is that the best way to job hunt is to jump into job hunting immediately. Doing this will cause you more stress because you haven't prepared yourself. True you may submit on jobs, but chances are you won't be putting your best foot forward. Instead take a few days to put yourself in the right frame of mind, organize your thoughts, develop a plan, and get prepared to put your best foot forward. A little preparation now will pay off big in the long run.

3
I WAS WHAT?

Politically correct feel-good euphemisms have invaded every corner of the workplace. Personnel actions are now so couched in vague language that one of the biggest questions former employees ask is, 'I was what?' Not from shock, but from confusion. This is compounded by employers who hide behind vague terminology afraid of anger, or worst of all – a lawsuit.

So here is the short version of an inexhaustibly long list of job loss terms:

A. Fired
This is also known as a dismissal. Basically your employer is requiring you to leave. Generally they believe you've done something wrong. A key component is that they are requiring you to leave; you don't actually want to leave. The day of your dismissal is generally the last day you're there. They don't want to drag things out and honestly, what type of work ethic would you have?
Depending on the state you live in you may or may not be eligible for unemployment. It's worth giving it a try.
There are two subtypes of termination that you need to be

aware of:
1. Terminated without prejudice: This means that you can be rehired at that company for the same type of job. You can even apply for and be hired back for the job you just left (it happens a lot more often than you'd think).
2. Terminated with prejudice: You are barred from being rehired at any similar job with that company. Generally you've done something and they don't want anything to do with you. Good news is that there are other fish in the sea and employers you can excel at.

B. Layoff

These are generally better received. Instead of you messing up (as in being fired) the forces of nature and/or economics messed up. If the economy tanks or your company goes bankrupt then everyone gets to chalk it up as bad (fill in the blank). Good news is that being laid off does not count against you in any way. Bad news, you still lost your job.

At-will employment and you, remember that 75 percent of working people are temporary and the other 25 percent are in denial. Most of the United States workforce is comprised of at-will employees. This means that your company can come to you at any time and let you go for almost any reason. These reasons can be stated or unstated (so vague you can't figure then out) and may be wholly unrelated to anything you've done (both performance and ethics based).

If you were asked to leave during your initial probationary period than you may be allowed to say you were laid off depending on how your official release paperwork (maintained by Human Resources not necessarily your former manager) is worded. Have a copy of it handy to refer to.

C. Termination by Mutual Agreement

Why would an employee agree to be terminated? One of the clearest examples is that of a contract employee. They sign a contract to work for a set period of time after which they can leave.

Another common example is a job with a mandatory retirement age. It's arguable if the employee is totally in agreement with the termination. However it's generally a well-known aspect of the job so by entering into that job they are giving a form of consent. An example of this are airline pilots. You don't see any sixty year old airline pilots because they are forced to retire at an earlier age.

Finally there are forced resignations which allow an employee to exit gracefully rather than be humiliated by an (impending) firing.

D. The Subtle Nudge

Some companies don't want to deal with all the unpleasantries and hassle that comes with laying off and firing employees. Endeavoring to make things easier for themselves they resort to giving employees subtle nudges hoping they'll leave on their own.

Subtle nudges are changes in your working conditions designed to make you work life as unpleasant as possible. This includes changing shifts, openly hostile work environments, and/or relocation to other cities/states.

If you quit on your own there's a very good chance you won't be eligible for unemployment. If your employer is caught for constructive dismissal (the legal term for tactics designed to bring about your resignation or quitting) they can be prosecuted in some jurisdictions. The problem is the time and expense spent trying to prove it.

Why All This Matters

Not only will your ability to receive unemployment be affected, but so will what you have to disclose on a job asking for a reason application. Always look! Even if there is a space on the application look to see if it's a required answer (usually in bold or with an * next to it) if it is required than answer with your prepared answer. If it's not required than don't answer. If at all possible you want to answer this during an interview not on some computer application.

Closing Note

While it is important to clarify what happened, remember that it is not a label that defines you. You still have all your skills and talents despite what a piece of paper or one job says about you. Being unemployed/fired/etc. is a label describing (accurately or inaccurately) an event or condition not a statement about you as a person. Encapsulate what happened into a response you can give in interviews, but remember that what happened is small compared to the big picture. The more you focus on it the more other people (including interviewers) will focus on it. Would you rather people focus on the years of accomplishments you have or on one blip? It's up to you.

4
UNEMPLOYMENT: THE LONG WAIT

What is Unemployment?

Unemployment Insurance, commonly referred to simply as Unemployment is a joint-program funded and run by both state and federal governments with the aim of providing temporary help to unemployed workers.

Every state is responsible for administering their own unemployment programs as long as these programs follow federal government guidelines. As a result every state has its own regulations as well as the federal government regulations. It's a dizzying array of regulations.

Who Gets Unemployment?

In general you have to have been unemployed through no fault of your own. Taken literally this means that if you were fired you're not eligible, but unemployment insurance is rarely a literal process. It never hurts to apply. The worst thing is that you're denied.

How Are Unemployment Benefits Determined?

You have to have worked in order to eligible. You can't draw from the fund until after you've contributed to it. The general rule is that your benefits are determined by how much you worked during the previous 52 weeks (1 year). It is important to note that the count is started from when you apply or the last day of your last job depending on your state and is counted backwards.

Anyone who has been on unemployment will tell you that you don't get an amount equal to what you had been making. Instead you get a percentage of what you had been making, how this percentage is determined remains a mystery for the most part. In addition every state sets a maximum benefit limit meaning that once you reach a certain level it doesn't matter if you make more, you're not getting any more.

No Such Thing As Free Money

Unemployment benefits are taxed, both state and federal. When you receive your benefits you have two options to choose from:

1. Have the taxes taken out of your benefit checks. Pro: You won't be stuck with a tax bill come next April. Con: The amount of your weekly check will be smaller since the taxes are being withheld.
2. Receive your full benefits now and pay the taxes in April when you pay your taxes. Pros: You receive the full amount of your benefits now when you need it most. Cons: You'll be stuck with a tax bill in April.

By the way, if you elect to wait until April to pay the taxes don't even think of not declaring (or "forgetting") the income. You will be caught as even the most dysfunctional government will catch on and then you'll have to face fines, fees and the possibility of jail time. All are far worse than grumbling and paying the taxes.

The Waiting Game

You should apply for unemployment as soon as you can. Wait until you have all the necessary information and then apply. 'Why bother to apply right away?' you ask. The reason is receiving your unemployment benefits is a game of hurry up and wait. Hurry up to apply so that you can wait. And wait you shall.

The length of time you'll wait depends on a number of factors, many of which are beyond your control. If your former employer delays in responding to requests for information made by the unemployment bureau your claim will be delayed. In addition the worse the economy is the longer the delay can be. This is because the state will have more claims to process and the same or less money to process them. These and a host of other reasons can cause your claim to be delayed. Delays can range from a few days (which you probably won't notice) to weeks that stretch into months (yes you read that right, months).

Many states have a waiting period as well. You have to be unemployed for a certain number of weeks (usually four to six) before you collect unemployment benefits. The idea being that you have to really be unemployed not just between jobs. If you can submit your claim during this period do it. You'll be waiting during this time anyway.

Honesty… Many Shades of Grey

You work hard; you pay your taxes, and generally consider yourself to be an honest person. It's something you pride yourself, it's also something that could cost you your unemployment claim. But if you're not honest you could get caught and then you'd be in a world of trouble. So what's an honest person to do? I am in no way telling you that you should not be honest on your unemployment claim, you should be, but remembering that the point of the unemployment office is to delay or deny your claim, it's important to know that honesty may end up costing you in the end.

One of the more common examples is the question you are asked every week you file a claim, "Was there are reason this week that you were unable to work?" Honesty would say that if your sister died and you went to her funeral, or you were in the hospital having your appendix removed and you were unavailable for two days of the week, honesty would say that you mark yes. The problem is that if you are honest you're claim for that week will be red flagged and an interview requested. Your claim is held up until that interview which may be several weeks away. Meanwhile your honesty means that you wait, without your claim. So while you shouldn't lie you could employ some creative thinking strategies. You can look for a job while waiting for that flight to your sister's funeral (not that you have to do much looking, but some would work), or while you are recovering from surgery you can look at the want ads. It's a grey area and up for you to decide what to do about it.

The Interview

Unemployment interviews are not fun. The good news is that in most cases the interview is done over the phone so you can relax at home and don't have to get dressed up and go to some office. In addition since the unemployment office has a massive number of interviews they have to get through, your interview will be very short (over ten minutes is rare). The bad news is that you might have to go through more than one interview.

Your eligibility (and payments) won't be determined until after the interview(s). Be nice to the person interviewing you, they can make or break your claim. You'll be assigned a date and time for your interview. Do everything you can to keep that appointment. If something comes up and you have to reschedule call and do so as soon as it is possible. Do not just ignore the appointment. If you have to change your appointment your new time will be at a later dates. This delays a determination about your benefits. Rescheduling for an earlier date ranges from impossible to not even allowed.

And That's Just the Beginning

Keeping track of all the jobs you've applied for as well as any interviews you've had is not just for your records. The unemployment bureau wants to see that you're actively trying to get a new job. You will be asked to provide lists (and proof) that your job hunting. You'll supply this proof via a mail in form, online form or over the phone (not as common). Keeping good records as you job hunt makes this process easier.

You, Your Job Hunt and the Unemployment Office

Unemployment benefits are not free and they come with a host of strings. You have to meet the requirements set forth by the Unemployment Office every week in order to be eligible. It's the ultimate Big Brother scenario. So what exactly do you have to do?

1. Look for Work

    This seems like a no-brainer, but not only do people forget this, but leave it up to the government to complicate a seemingly simple process. First of all you have to look for both full and part-time work. In addition "looking for work" isn't really accurate. You can't just cruise through the job boards once a day and call it a day. Instead you have to apply for jobs.

2. Unions and You

    If you belong to a union or you work in an occupation with a union, you are required to be a member of that union and use those union resources to help you locate a job.

3. Be Ready to Work

    Every week you have to be ready, willing and able to work. Of course emergencies arise and for one or several days you may not be able to fulfill this requirement. Be prepared that whatever reason you tell the unemployment office had better be really good. They've heard it all before, have really good bull shit detectors, and in many cases are looking for reasons to deny your claim.

Other Factors to Consider

A. School

    If you stared school or began any type of training you need to report it because it can impact your unemployment

benefits.
B. Did You Refuse Work?
Always a bad idea. If you're offered work of any type, it's expected that you'll take it (no matter how weird). Refuse it and your claim will be held up until an interview can be arranged to "clarify" the situation.
C. Did You Earn Any Money?
You're supposed to report every single cent you make (seriously if you find change on the ground the unemployment office and the IRS probably want to know about it). Don't report income (intentionally or unintentionally) and if your caught the penalties are astronomical. So don't lie about your income. (That being said if you asked most people who are of have ever been on unemployment to be honest at some point in time someone has given them a few bucks to help out. Since no paperwork was signed it's not likely to be reported.). The decision is up to you.
D. Ending Your Claim
Hopefully you're doing this because you found a job. Congratulations! Do not end your claim when you receive an offer, either verbal or written. Wait until the end of your first full day at your new job. You want to make sure that it is a real job, you actually want to work there, and that it will be a long-term (or last the specified term). Once you've confirmed this cancel your unemployment benefits. Delay doing this and you could end up being overpaid. Sounds good until you realize that you will have to pay it back plus penalties and interest. You may also be disqualified from receiving benefits in the future.
E. Reopening Your Claim
So you took the job and cancelled your claim, just like you were supposed to, only to have the job go south, evaporate or otherwise disappear are a few weeks. In this case many

states will let you reopen your previous claim (often online) rather than going through the hassle of opening a whole new claim.

Other General Information

Exactly how unemployment benefits are paid out varies from state to state. Although some states still send out paper checks in this era of rampant mail theft and fraud more states are opting for debit cards that are automatically reloaded. In theory this makes the process easier, but if you lose your debit card getting a new one can be a nightmare.

A final note: This chapter is intended to provide general information about how unemployment works. Not every statement will apply to every person or situation. As with everything in this book (and in life) take what works and what applies to you and leave the rest.

5
MANY PATHS

There are many benefits to losing your job. Yes I said benefits. Were you in a job you didn't like, but just couldn't get around to leaving? Often losing your job allows you to become unstuck (through rather abruptly) pried from a toxic environment and thrust into a whole world that opens up before you like a vast plain. For many people these options include changing careers. A surprising number of people ended up in their current careers by accident, in desperation, or because they were pressured to. In losing their job they gain their freedom.

If you want to change careers (or at least explore the possibility) how do you go about it?

1. Find What You Love (or at least like) to Do: Sounds simple but a lot of people honestly don't know what they love to do. Daydream. Think what you love to do, what you've always wanted to do. At this stage put no limits on yourself.
2. What did you want to be as a kid? Jot down notes no matter how random or impossible they seem.
3. Pay Attention: In your daily life notice what intrigues you, what you like, what captures your imagination. Once again

at this stage note everything. What seems insignificant now may end up being essential later on.

4. Testing: Taking a career aptitude test can yield surprising results. People often laugh at the results (tree farmer?), but these tests can yield a large list of occupations, many of which you may have never thought of. These tests don't tell you what career you're guaranteed to be successful at, rather they point to careers that match your personality and aptitude. Think of it as online dating. You're not guaranteed of finding "the one"; instead you're presented with the most likely candidates. The theory is that if you're in a career that matches your personality and aptitude, you're likely to be happy; therefore you're likely to be more successful. There are many places that offer these tests for low or no cost so it's worth exploring around. When you take these tests remember that you only get out of them what you put into them. There is no way to fail these tests and faking answers only makes the process useless because you won't get accurate results.

5. Define Success: Find out how you define success. Is it a tons of money? Fame? Success? Or is it something else? Happy family? Fulfilling work? Figure out what defines success for you. An important part of satisfaction in life and in your career is figuring out what success means to you and then finding a career that helps to meet that for you.

6. Research: Learn about the types of jobs that interest you. The Internet is a tremendous resource but also look at trade magazines to get an idea. Another tremendous resource can be job shadowing. This is like an internship but without the lengthy commitment. It requires effort on your part as you have to find someone in your interested career and develop enough of a relationship to ask them if you can job shadow. The benefit is that you'll get a look at what the job is really like day-to-day.

7. Education: Find out if there are any specialized licenses or training needed. In addition look to see if you already have skills and expertise that can be used in lieu of formal education. Going back to school doesn't necessarily mean attending full-time and accumulating mountains of debt. Explore all your options before diving in.
8. Plan: Switching careers will mean a commitment of both time and money. Make sure to plan carefully so that you will have a strong idea of what you're working for as well as how you are going to get there. Part of developing a plan is to make it reasonable. If you plan to get through college in one year you're setting yourself up for failure. Be realistic about both time and money.
9. Ask (and answer) Why? Make sure that your new career is something you want to do not something you're jumping into out of desperation. One good question to ask is if you're attracted to this 'new' career solely because of the money you might make or because some economic forecaster says it's a hot career. Know what's important and stick to it.
10. Be Prepared to Be Patient: Changing careers takes time and lots of planning. While it is fun to fantasize about what your new business will look like (if that's your dream) before you get lost in picking out business cards and imagining yourself on the cover of a magazine be prepared and be patient. Take classes in business, study up on your chosen profession, do everything in order to prepare yourself for success.

    Above all be patient. Changing careers can be very rewarding, but 'rebranding' yourself takes time. Just as it took time to establish yourself in your past profession it will take time to establish yourself in your new profession. Be prepared that when you start you will be making far less than what you had been making (possibly even none). Be prepared and plan for this so that it doesn't come as a shock to you.

No matter what it's still work. "Do what you love and you'll never work a day in your life" is only partially true. You will always be working but if you're doing what you love at the end of a hard day's work you'll love what you've done.

6
ORGANIZING YOUR JOB HUNT TO MAINTAIN YOUR SANITY

The common adage is that looking for a full-time job is a full-time job and just as a full-time job can make you question your sanity so can job hunting. Seemingly endless days of filling out applications are only the start. Interviews where you get yourself psyched up and stressed out only to be let down by rejection, try even the most well-balanced person. So how do you maintain your sanity while job hunting? Believe it or not there are a number of simple (and cheap) you can do to survive (and thrive!) while job hunting.

Organization is key to a successful and sane job hunt. Having the information and supplies you need handy and organized will help eliminate stress and wasted time. Imagine not being organized. You start off the morning ready to job hunt, but first you have to clear a space to sit. Then you have to turn on your computer and locate your mouse which has disappeared under a mountain of paperwork. One hour into your job hunting day and you haven't begun to job hunt. Still you get started and today's your lucky day because you find a perfect job. You click to apply and have to create an account. You fill out the form only to get an error message that you already have an account. Thing is you don't remember the login information. 'It was on a yellow piece of paper', you think looking at yellow pieces of paper scattered everywhere. The next twenty minutes are spent digging through paperwork before you give up in frustration and spend the next fifteen minutes going through the steps to recover your login information. At this rate you'll be lucky to apply for one job before lunch!

An organized job hunt does not have to involve any fancy high-tech, or expensive supplies. Remember while you're job hunting you're also trying to keep expenses low so look around to see what you have already that you can use. Tailor your system to meet your needs. My system involves my computer and printer, a thumb drive (for file backup), a legal pad, one sheet protector (not necessary, but I had one lying around so I use it), and an assortment of pens, highlighters and markers. That's it. It's all the stuff I already had on hand. Throughout this chapter you'll see different tips and techniques to help you organize your job hunt. Use what works, modify to make other things work and ignore what doesn't work for you. What's important is that you develop a system that works for you and if what you're doing isn't working than change it. This isn't rocket science (unless you happen to be a rocket scientist).

Your Resume

There are literally hundreds of books and thousands of websites that will explain in excruciating detail how to write (or craft if the author's feeling fancy) a resume.

If you've never written a resume than take the time to learn and have several trusted people take a look at it for their honest feedback. I've never been a big fan of resume writing services, but the disclaimer is that I've never used one. I've just seen (and helped fix) resumes that people spent money having other people write. I'm in favor of writing your own resume for a number of reasons. First, the purpose of your resume is to sell you and you know you better than anybody else. Secondly, many low-budget resume writers just plug your information into a generic template. A generic template may not be the best format for you. Third, you don't have money to burn right now so forking it over to someone when writing it yourself is ridiculously simple seems like a waste of money. Forth, although initially writing your resume may take a few hours, once it's done any updating and changing you want to make now or in the future becomes relatively easy and free.

If you already have a resume make sure to dust it off and update it. Every decade or so the job hunting world decides to change the "in" format of what an ideal resume looks like. Poke around online to figure out what the current format is and update yours accordingly. Make sure to add your most recent employer. Don't forget to make sure your contact information is current and to add any new skills, publications, and achievements.

Cover Letters

This general idea goes for cover letters although it's best to think of your cover letter as a template rather than a form. The wording and structure of your cover letter won't vary much, but specifics and anything listed in the job description that you want to highlight you will have to change. Think of it as an advanced fill-in-the-blank (or Mad Libs game). You want to make it personal and tailor it to the specific job you're applying for, but you don't want to spend your entire day writing each cover letter from scratch. All that being said you will occasionally run across those awesome jobs that seem to demand a totally unique cover letter. By all means go ahead!

One way to think of it is to create different paragraphs each highlighting a particular skill or quality. Move them around on your cover letter putting them in the order that you want. Each cover letter will have a different combination of paragraphs, but you won't waste time writing each one from scratch every time.

Beginning Your Job Hunt

Once you have these documents created save them! Save several copies! Print copies for your records! Not only will they be a handy reference, but if your computer melts down or your thumb drive is given a trip down the toilet by your child, you will have back-ups so you won't have to start from scratch.

Now you're ready to job hunt. This is where I explain how I job hunt on the cheap. In the margin of the legal pad I write the current date. As I submit on jobs (actual submissions only) I write the job title, the company, the job number, and the submission confirmation number. The goal is to make all of this information fit on one line. This way I can simply count the number of lines in any given day to see how many jobs I applied for. If I hear back that I didn't get the interview or job I cross the line with that job off. If I hear back that I did get an interview than I highlight the line with that job submission (and congratulate myself). The next day I put the new date down and continue.

But what about job descriptions you ask. Job descriptions can be tediously long and if you print out every one you'll end up with stacks of paper everywhere. Not cost-effective, not environmentally friendly, and fairly futile. This is where copy and paste on your computer saves you. At the beginning of the day start a new file (Notepad is great, but any similar program works just as well). As you apply for jobs copy the job descriptions from the websites and paste them into your blank document. Save this periodically as well as at the end of the day. To keep things simple I usually name each file with the date of that day's listings. This way you have the job descriptions if you get the interview, but you're not wasting ink and paper. If there's one that you need, say for an interview you can print that specific one out. The next day start a new file and go on from there.

As you job hunt many websites will have you create accounts. You'll have to create usernames and passwords and for some reason almost none of them will ask for the same thing. The result is a laundry list of websites, usernames and passwords. I keep all mine on a sheet of paper inside a sheet protector (yes it's not the most secure, so I'm not really recommending this method, it's the lesson not the method that matters here). The point is you have to develop some way of keeping this information handy otherwise you'll end up wasting huge amounts of time recovering lost passwords and usernames.

The good news is that many of these sites will let you create and save a general application for future use. The bad news, initially setting up these applications can be a time consuming pain. In addition if you choose to let the site fill in the application using your resume (importing your resume) you then need to check your application to make sure that it's a) complete, b) accurate, and c) that the website actually put the correct information in the correct field. It can take anywhere from fifteen minutes (on a smaller site, or one that's well set-up) to several hours (for a massive site like LinkedIn or usajobs.gov) to set-up a profile. Don't forget that these sites take maintenance, an old out-of-date profile and resume may actually damage your job search. In addition for many sites you only get out of them what you put in. It's effort up front that may pay off later.

Job Boards

Don't look at just one. Here it's almost a more the merrier approach at least in the beginning. The large job boards (indeed.com, monster.com, etc.) are good at catching a wide variety of postings. Specialty job boards such as idealist.com for socially-conscious job seekers or aerotek.com for science and engineering jobs are great resources. In addition don't forget academia (the easiest way to search college and university jobs is to go directly to those schools) or government (usajobs.gov is the central posting for all federal government jobs). Craigslist can be another source of local jobs. I've heard stories of people landing jobs on Craigslist. However my personal experience is that Craigslist is better at landing short-term and temporary jobs than anything long-term. Still a few minutes once a day scrolling through the postings is entertaining at the very least.

Now you've got your space, your supplies and your paperwork

… stop procrastinating and start job hunting! The reason it's called job hunting is because it's an active process, you have to put forth the effort to gain the results.

Set a plan … and stick to it. Just as not doing anything won't land you a job, frantic hunting can actually be counterproductive. You may be one of those people thinking 'I'm going to job hunt twelve hours a day seven days a week without stopping until I have a job'. I know because I've said that before. Almost everyone I know has said that at one point. Problem is this plan backfires. You get burnt out, begin making stupid mistakes, and may even make yourself physically ill. Instead set a plan.

Companies rarely post jobs when they aren't open for business. Really, do you honestly think one lonely human resources assistant is in the office at 2am on a Sunday? Concentrate your job hunting for times when businesses are actually open. For most people this means Monday-Friday from 8am-5pm. I amend this to be Monday-Friday from 9am-6pm. Not only do I get to sleep in a bit, but I still catch the first postings of the day and have time after the close of business to play catch-up on any last minute postings.

When you are job hunting be actively job hunting. Don't play Solitaire or chat on Facebook, your job is to get a job.

Breaks

These are up to your temperament but make sure to take them. Get up, walk around, get some fresh air, get a snack, whatever you do take a few moments to relax, you'll come back to your job hunt refreshed and ready to dive back in.

Downtime

When your job hunting is done for the day or the week, put it aside. This can be very difficult. You may find yourself thinking 'I shouldn't be taking any time off when I'm unemployed' or 'It's wrong to feel happy about anything right now'. Combat these thoughts. You've worked hard job hunting and you need a break.

Most companies don't post nights and weekends anyway. And most importantly getting out and enjoying life helps to put things in perspective and provide a source of joy.

Keeping it All Together

As your job hunt wears on (and with the average job hunt measured in months this can be a long time), depression, despair, anxiety, and hopelessness can weigh heavily on you (not to mention a host of other negative emotions). So how do you keep your spirits up during this time?

Besides keeping a regular schedule and taking up a hobby (both ideas discussed elsewhere in this book) there are some other simple techniques.

1. Take Care of Yourself. Get exercise (if you've ever wanted to start now's the perfect time!). This is even more effective when combine with being outside.
2. Be Social. Talking and meeting with friends and other people provides interaction and a source of support. A bonus is that this can qualify as networking.
3. Be Active. Volunteer in the community. Nothing compares to the satisfaction that comes from helping others.
4. Counseling. If you fell that you've reached the point where your depression or other feelings are impairing you, or if you just want to talk to someone, many communities have free and low-cost counseling options. In addition your community may also have discussion and support groups for job seekers.
5. Be Kind to Yourself. You're going to have bad days ("I only applied for one job!"). The key is not to panic, realize this is natural, and celebrate the successes no matter how small.

7

NEW BEGINNINGS:
GETTING IN THE "HIRE ME" MINDSET

Job hunting is a game and like any game winning rarely depends solely on trying harder or longer. Instead much of the success you have in job hunting comes from how you play the game. Your job hunting strategy could well-determine your success.

Case in point: Sending out mountains of applications all personally addressed to "Whom It May Concern" wastes a lot of your time and energy. Taking the time to personalize (in some small way) your applications shows; a. that you are a real person and not a computer indiscriminately blasting out applications, b. in theory you have actually read the job description; and c. you actually care. Any, all, or none of these may actually be true, but part of the job hunting game involves large amounts of doing things because that's just the way they're done. You can spend all your time trying to change the system and likely get nothing for it, or you can go with it and get a job.

Good news for you is that an essential component of winning the job hunt game is your mindset. The confident "Hire Me" mindset will do wonders. Just look at most politicians. Their entire careers are built on selling themselves with such an overwhelming amount of confidence that their Hire Me/Elect Me mentality gets them elected time and again even if they have absolutely no demonstrated ability to do the job. How is that the case?

Confidence, potential employees have a "Hire Me" mindset that they are able to convince millions of people that they must be elected for this job.

Good news for you is that you're not a politician. You don't have millions of voters deciding your future. You have a handful of people (the person who weeds through the applications, the person/people who interview you, your future boss, and your future coworkers – bearing in mind these might all be the same person) deciding your fate. Bad news, if one of these people doesn't like you your job gets all that much harder.

'But I got the interview so they obviously want to hire me, right?' No. Remember that they are interviewing many people. As much as they are looking for reasons to hire you, they are also looking for reasons not to hire you because that narrows the field and makes it easier for them to decide. You have to sell the interview committee on you as the perfect future employee.

The first step is to know the current job market. There's a reason everyone refers to job hunting as a jungle you have to hunt through. Blindly charge ahead and you're likely to expend a lot of energy and make very little progress. Step back, look at the market, figure out what you want, what's in demand, and how to make the two fit. Do that and you'll have a map through the jungle.

See the end. Long before you reach the end envision what it looks like. Not only will this keep you focused, it will help you see what steps you can take to realize your goal.

The Think Method

Growing up my father would start a task me would first sit down and employ the Think Method as he called it. I would always laugh as he'd sit in a chair and stare off into space for what seemed like forever. Occasionally he'd make a note on some paper, sometimes he'd mutter to. This would happen every time for every task and the impatient child I was would harass the future employer to hurry up and start. After what seemed liked forever he'd stand up and announce that he'd figured out how to do the task. The actual doing of the task would go very fast and with very few problems. When I was a child it seemed like magic, as an adult I understand it was due to the Think Method. This story illustrates a very important aspect of job-hunting. Unless you think about what you want from a job and think of how you're going to get it your chances of getting it remain low. How will you know if you get your dream job if you don't know what your dream job is?

The Think Method is what my father calls it, but many people know it as visualization. The basic concept is the same, how do you know when you've found 'it' if you don't know what 'it' is? Taking the time to stop and figure out what you want and what your goal is will help you to figure out if a career/job offer/job posting is what you want. An example of this is that you may want a job where you can effect change but you are private and quiet. Knowing this can help you decide that being a policy researcher may suit you better than a non-profit fundraiser. Both jobs satisfy your passion but one better suits your ideal work environment.

One way to help you visualize is to think about and write down things you did and did not like about your former jobs (not just your most recent. Pick the top few likes and dislikes from this list to give you an idea about what is important to you).

The next step is to visualize what your ideal job would be. Imagine what a day in the life of your dream job would be, what would a week be like? What would your office look like, where would it be located? Would you even have an office? Understand that your new job may not look exactly like what you envision but this gives you an ideal from which to work.

The Think Method and visualization won't get you very far. It's easiest to think of them as a roadmap, they'll point you in the right direction but they won't actually drive the car. Only action, action on your part can do that. My father's Think Method was useless until he put his thoughts into action. You can visualize your dream job as much as you want, but until you put forth the effort to find the job there is virtually no chance of it ever becoming reality.

Look Before You Leap

Many people when faced with a sudden job loss flip into survival mode… and stay there. As with anything in life a bit of survival mode is good. It allows you to make immediate plans and help you accurately assess your situation, but you can't and you shouldn't exist in this mode long-term. You can't because while survival mode helps you in the short run, paradoxically in the long run this level of stress wears on you both physically and psychologically. You becomes worn down and prone to sickness. Your concentration also suffers as fatigue takes over and you become unable to focus and concentrate.

In addition you shouldn't be in survival mode long-term because it can negatively affect your judgment and decision-making. You'll find yourself making rash decisions based on fear ("I'll never find another job here I have to move now!"), decisions you'll later regret. This is because decisions based in fear are usually rushed into because you want to find a quick way of dealing with all the uncomfortable emotions you feel. You've lost your job and along with your fear you may feel shame, guilt, anxiety, sadness, and frustration. These are feelings that no one likes to experience, but rushing blindly into a decision without stopping to examine it fully may find you worse off. Believe it or not there are worse things than being unemployed.

On the other hand you may find yourself paralyzed with fear staring blankly at the wall not even knowing what to do next or where to start. Your paralyzed state renders you incapable of doing anything and it is highly unlikely that job offers will land in your inbox without you doing something.

Combating Boredom

Job hunting is boring. There's no way around it. Your location doesn't matter, sooner or later you'll get bored of seeing the same people at the coffee shop, the same stacks of books at the library, or the same walls of your house. It's enough to make you go insane. I job hunt with the television on for noise and joke that I could be a lawyer based on the number of Law & Order episodes I've watched. The problem with being bored is that it will lead you to make careless mistakes ("Wait! Did I put the correct phone number down?!"). In addition you can forget how to talk to people. If your only social interaction is with your pet or the checker at the grocery store your polished professional communication skills can get a bit rusty. So how do you maintain your polish so you can really shine at interviews?

Get Out There!

Carry on conversations with people. If your shame at being unemployed is holding you back, remember that most people have been unemployed at some point. The hilarious stories people would tell me about being fired/laid off/unemployed made me laugh, lifted my spirits, and in part led to the creation of this book. In the future when you look back you'll probably laugh at this point in your life, so why not practice now?

Job hunting is a full-time job but that doesn't mean it has to consume you. Many museums have free days in the middle of the week, take an afternoon to explore one. Enjoy the fresh air of a park. Just get out there! "But I have to job hunt! I don't have time (or deserve to) have any fun!" you may cry.

Nonsense! First of all everyone deserves to have fun, I'm pretty sure it's a basic human right (if not it should be). Secondly, having a little fun now and then will actually make you a more effective job hunter. One of the best ways to cure the monotony of job hunting is to take a break from it. By doing so you'll be able to relax, refocus and when you return to job-hunting you'll be more effective.

Know The Gatekeeper

Your interviewer is not the enemy, rather they are the gatekeeper determining if you're worthy to pass. They are also real people and there's a very good chance they're nervous too. You don't want to beat them, you want to join them.

Image is (almost) Everything

Part of being confident is presenting yourself as confident, capable, and professional. This means a clean and neat suit for every interview even if it's the blistering heat of summer. Use as much deodorant as you need, then use some more. There are countless webpages and articles on how to dress for interviews. Read them. Follow them. "But, I hate wearing suits", you whine. I know because I do. To me interview suits are akin to medieval torture devices. Still, if you want the job then you have to dress the part.

When to Talk, When to Shut Up

An odd thing happens when people get nervous and lose their confidence. Some people clam up, say nothing and give one word answers like they're being questioned by the police. The other group of people do the opposite. They start talking and won't shut up. You swear they don't even pause to talk a breath. So what are you to do? Practice, practice, practice. Practice not only in mock interviews, but in other social situations. Listen to how much you talk, or don't talk and see how other people react. If you find yourself talking too much practice active listening. Don't respond until the other person has finished speaking (this also shows you respect what they're saying). Then organize your thoughts. Instead of saying the eight things that come to your mind in an unorganized dump, focus on the two or three most important and/or unique points you want to make and make them in two or three sentences. This will also show that you have the ability to organize and prioritize your thoughts.

Pre-Interview Confidence

Congratulations, you got the interview! Now you're sitting in the waiting area right before the interview begins and those nagging thoughts start destroying your self-confidence. How do you keep those thoughts at bay so you can go with confidence into your interview?

1. Plan. Plan. Plan. (and then plan some more)

    Don't be on time for an interview, be early. Allow plenty of time for traffic and parking. Once you're parked make sure you're in the right location (South Broadway vs. North Broadway is a big difference).

2. Plan Beforehand

    Make sure to have several copies of your resume handy. Take pens, a clipboard, and paper. Filling out a job application with a beat-up borrowed pen balanced on your knee is not the way to start. Now a word about cell phones. If you must take it in (I prefer to leave mine in the car just to be on the safe side), off is the only way to go. It's amazing how loud a phone on vibrate can sound. Not to mention how distracting.

3. Think Positive

    Learn to immediately counteract any negative thoughts with positive ones. Having a hard time thinking of positive ones on the moment? Write down several on a card and stash it somewhere handy like your wallet. Refer to it as necessary.

4. Practice the Pitch … and responses

    Go over your sales pitch about you in your head. Not only does this boost your confidence it helps assure that you won't be at a loss for words to start with. In addition practice your response to the questions you know are coming. You'll be calmer.

5. Research

    Know about the company, what they do and what they're

known for. This conveys genuine interest on your part.
6. Visualization

    This works for a lot of people so it's worth a try. Imagine the interview going astoundingly well and getting the job offer. Fill in as much detail as possible. The idea being your trying to create the reality you want.

In The Interview

No matter how much preparation you've done there will still come that moment where the interview actually starts. How do you handle that?

1. Step by Step.

    Shake hands with everyone, make eye contact. Sit down and take a deep breath. Don't rush to start the interview, take a moment to compose and put everything else out of your mind.

2. Slow Time

    This is not a game show where you have to rush to give the answer. In fact a reflective pause before answering shows that you are preparing a thoughtful answer rather than blurting out the first thing that comes to your mind.

3. Ask Questions

    Believe it or not an interview is not a one-sided interrogation. Be prepared with a few well-thought out questions for the interview. An especially interesting question is to ask the interviewer what they believe to be your greatest strengths and weaknesses about doing this job. But don't leave the answer hanging! Counter all the weaknesses they list. It's bold but it shows a great deal of confidence on your part. It also gives you an idea on where you stand for the job.

4. Anticipate Questions and Volunteer Answers to Them

    There are certain questions that you know you're going to be asked. Questions about being part of a team and your strengths and weaknesses (usually three of each) are standard (no I don't know why because everybody hates them and people's answers are so rehearsed that asking has become a pointless exercise). So be proactive and answer the question before it is asked. A large part of successful interviewing is attitude. Interviewers (great ones) are not passive interrogators. Ask questions back and volunteer information (positive only!).

5. Be Likable

   People hire people that they like. Being liked can overcome many other shortcomings. You don't have to be a shameless brownnoser, but pay attention to how people perceive you! Body language and nonverbal communication play a huge role in this. Being the type of person who looks like they could beat up people in a dark alley may make employers for a youth camp think twice. Ask you friends how they would describe you and then ask yourself if it would be attractive to a future employer.

6. Ask For the Job

   As you're leaving the interview express how much you like the company and position. Then ask for the job. It may seem obvious that since you just did the interview you're interested in the job, but actually asking for the job conveys your enthusiasm, and enthusiasm is great.

7. Failure Is an Option, but It Will Never Happen

   You won't get every job you interview for. In fact the statistic has been floated around that for every six interviews you go on you'll net one job offer. Putting aside the fact that most statistics are meaningless you will never fail at a job interview if you view it as a learning experience. You learn what worked and what didn't work to be better prepared for the next interview. This accumulated experience is more valuable than any advice you will ever receive regarding job hunting.

The Importance of Emotional Intelligence

Emotional Intelligence, or EI, is not dependent on being social and outgoing. Being an introvert or being shy can actually be an asset. This is because Emotional Intelligence is your ability to accurately assess other people's needs. As a job-hunter you may have amazing skills like being a surgeon, but if you're applying to be an aircraft designer (I'm purposefully using extreme to illustrate the point) how well do you think you're going to able to meet the needs of the aerospace design company? Chances are not well.

Another point to keep in mind is that during your job hunt your focus is on your needs. 'What type of job and employer are you looking for?' is your main focus.

An interviewer doesn't really care about all that. An interviewer cares about the needs of the company, how that position fulfills them, and how well you will fill that position.

Emotional Intelligence is your ability to be a chameleon, reading between the lines and what is not said to figure out what qualities and criteria the interviewer is looking for. Having done that you have to show how well you fill them.

An interview is not to make you feel good it's to make the interviewer feel good about hiring you.

8
ETHICS, LOYALTY, MANNERS AND OTHER LITTLE THINGS

Losing your job changes your perspective making you think that the world has lost all sense of loyalty, that business ethics are dead, manners don't count and that all common decency left the world. As tempting as it is to think this is the case such an attitude is not conducive to a job seeker.

Ethics

Business ethics is usually an oxymoron only joked at by late night talk show comedians. It's one thing to see news stories of corrupt business owners, it's another to have their actions affect you personally. How are you supposed to react when you've done everything right only to be the victim of circumstances beyond your control. Wanting to rant and rave about the injustices of the world is only natural.

But it won't get you a new job, in fact it will make potential employers run the other way. Even if a company acts in an unethical manner this does not give you permission to act unethically. When most people asked can tell you when a particular behavior is unethical, but in practice the lines can be blurred. Why should it matter?

Take scenario 1: Your employer is acting unethically by cutting corners in manufacturing. Since they're cheating the public you'd be right in stealing office supplies, right? Wrong. First of all there is the old adage that two wrongs don't make a right. Secondly if you're fired for stealing office supplies all that will go on your record is that you stole from the company. So when you look for work and are asked why you were fired you'll have to answer that it was for theft and unethical conduct. Any potential employer won't care about your justification; a charge of theft on your record will kill almost every job offer. So what did you gain? Likely your former unethical company went on with business as usual and you now find yourself in a very difficult position (by the way in a scenario such as this it is very unlikely that you would be eligible for unemployment either).

Unethical conduct also includes selling or telling of company secrets. At most companies it is routine to have new employees sign a stack of paperwork. Included in that paperwork (which almost no one reads) are usually agreement prohibiting you from revealing company or trade secrets. Ignoring this while you work at that company can get you fired and leave you facing legal action. But what about after you leave? Those agreements are still in force. Telling or selling company secrets can subject you to prosecution even through you no longer work at a particular company. In fact once you leave a company your actions and what you say may be even more scrutinized more. Disgruntled former employees are ripe for spilling company secrets.

You have to prove yourself to be above what has happened to you. It's the hallmark of a mature employee and the type of employee other companies what to hire.

Loyalty

Loyalty has all but disappeared in the modern workplace. Many older workers remember a time when you started working for a company right out of school and you stayed with them your entire life until you retired. They took care of you and you took care of them. Such loyalty as was seen in past generations is all but gone, but that does not mean that loyalty is dead.

Most people can think of a company they have worked with, even though they may not have felt loyal to the company there might have been a manager of a project that you felt particularly loyal to. You knew that person had your back and you reciprocated that.

Loyalty is still an important aspect of any business relationship. Modern employers don't expect that an employee they hire will stay with them forever. Most employees have several careers over the course of their lives and even more jobs. What employers really care about is that while you are working for them you are loyal to them. If you have divided loyalties in the workplace it is difficult to accomplish anything. While you are at work, be at work.

Part of this involves respect. Things as simple as showing up on time and not using company time to take personal calls make a big difference. One of employer's biggest complaints, and reasons they fire people are the misuse of company time to do personal business.

What if you know you're on the way out? The rumors have been circulating for weeks, the offices have been emptying, and you know you're one the way out, it's only a matter of time. Surely no one cares what you do, right? Wrong. Last impressions can matter more than first impressions. If the last thing everyone remembers about you was how you slacked off, came in late, left early, and spent your time making paper airplanes, that's not a good impression. These are the same people you might be asking for a recommendation, or asking to rehire you later on. Think how people will remember you and think if that's what you want them to remember.

What if you've made up your mind to leave and are actively job hunting? Loyalty (and respect) means that you do not take calls on company time. You schedule any interviews for time you are off. Be careful about scheduling lots of 'doctor's appointments' as managers will eventually catch on. Above all you are discrete. This is very important because you are looking for another job, you do not have another job. It's not a good idea to act like an ass and be disloyal because you're leaving a company only to have the offer fall through and have to remain at your current job. Nothing says disloyalty like flaunting your available status around the office.

That doesn't mean that if you are presently employed you shouldn't look for another job. By all means look away, apply, interview, and if you get a better offer by all means take it. Being loyal to yourself and your career is to be expected, but there is a way to be loyal to yourself and respectful to your employer.

Manners

We're not talking about high tea and meeting the queen, rather we're talking about basic common manners. These are manners that make a positive impression on an employer marking you as an adult and person it would be nice to work with.

The most basic rule of manners is the golden rule, 'treat others as you would have them treat you'. As part of your job hunt this involves putting yourself in your interviewers place. If you call them back and they answer sounding rushed asking if they can call you back in a few minutes, be polite and agree. Demanding that they drop everything they're doing and talk to you right then marks you as self-absorbed, demanding, and inflexible. Not the type of person they'll want to hire.

From before you walk in the door for your interview you're being assessed not only as a potential future employee, but also as a potential representative of the company. When you work for a company you are a representative of that company even when you're not at work. How you act during the interview process is being evaluated.

An essential component of good manners includes being on time for the interview, being polite and respectful to everyone in the office, and taking measures to ensure that your cell phone does not ring in the middle of the interview.

In addition good manners includes doing little things that mean a lot. What you do after an interview can help cinch the offer. Make sure to smile, shake everyone's hands, make a little bit of small talk (not too much because they're busy and have other things to do), and make sure to ask for the job. What then?

Write a Thank You Note. Very few job applicants write thank you notes after an interview. It used to be standard procedure, but is now relatively uncommon and that's one of the reasons you should always write a thank you note. It sets you apart from the crowd (in a good way), shows that you have manners and know proper business etiquette, plus it gives you another chance to ask for the job. When you write a thank you note remember to hand write it (with your best penmanship) and send through the mail the old-fashioned way. An email thank you note doesn't carry the same impact and is likely to get lost in an inbox.

Other Lost Things

It is easy to sit back and bemoan all of the traditional aspects of the job hunting world that have been lost crying about the way things used to be. Although the job hunting environment has changed it's not all for the bad. Stiff interviews in windowless stuffy rooms still happen, but more and more interviewers and learning that if they think outside the box when it comes to interview techniques they get a more genuine response.

Still no matter how much things change certain things will always stay the same. Good manners (adapted for a more politically correct environment) are always in fashion and will mark you as a serious candidate. Basics like good hygiene (You'd be surprised at how many people 'don't believe in deodorant' or 'ironed shirts'. Your personal beliefs aside if you believe in getting a job than you'd better develop a belief in these things). In addition a firm handshake goes a long way. This is something to practice since most people either have a vice grip (generally men) or a limp wrist (generally women).

The lifetime job is an old myth. Most people will change careers several times in their life and change jobs several more times. Changing jobs used to be the black mark of a job hopper, now it's the norm. In the current job market many career advisors say your goal should be able to stay in a job at least two years before changing, a string of jobs all under one year can be viewed as job hopping (through even this is up to interpretation). What is the other extreme? A job seeker who only has one job on their resume (but has been at that job for over a decade), can play up their loyalty and dedication, but also has to emphasize that their history of one job does not mean they are stuck in their ways and unable to adapt.

There is such things as a sure thing. This is a mistake that older workers often make. The thinking is that since you've got the job and you're doing a good job you're immune from being let go. No job is ever a sure thing and in the age of mergers and downsizing no one has a guaranteed job. Take this knowledge and instead of being paralyzed by fear, use it to make sure that you're prepared to be let go at any time. As much as possible an emergency fund while you're working. Most financial experts recommend at least three months' worth of expenses. In realist this is different, still aim for it realizing that any amount is better than none.

Something that isn't lost isn't the ideal job. That is mainly because there is no one ideal job. Every person has a different idea of the components of their job are. The important thing to understand is what is ideal for you. Find out what you simply must have in a work environment (things like respect and a living wage are usually on this list), what is nice (a quick commute, room for advancement, etc.), and things that fall further down the list (a nice office, a good retirement plan, etc.). Your ideal job fulfills as many of these things as possible. Beyond that it is also important to understand that the requirements of your ideal job will change throughout your career. Most twenty-something's just starting out are not as concerned with a company's retirement benefits as a forty-year old employee might be.

Making This Information Work for You

By now you've seen that some aspects of job hunting have changed and others look just the way they did fifty or sixty years ago. But all the information is just words on a page, it's what you do with that information is what matters.

A. Manners are always in style. Not high tea lifted pinky manners, but normal politeness, kindness and respect. Make these things part of your normal life and you'll be surprised at the reaction you get.
B. Find your ideal. Sure you can look for a job, any job that is a paycheck, and there is a time and place for that, but find out what your ideal is and make it a point to hunt for those jobs. Some jobs allow you to survive, other jobs allow you to thrive. Learn the difference.
C. Heed the wisdom of Hamlet "Above all to thine own self be true". When you're working at a company you have loyalty to that company. After you stop working at a company you still have an obligation to maintain confidentiality. But at the end of the day your loyalty is to yourself. Even the best company is ultimately focused on their best interests. You can't neglect yourself and your loyalty to yourself.
D. Jobs are transient. The downside is that you'll end up job hunting again (never a fun thing). The upside is that you're never stuck in a bad job, all things will end.
E. Spin is (almost) everything. Just as the wrong words said to the wrong people can ruin your chances at a particular job, the right words can make gaps, gray areas, and other questionable aspects of your employment history look a lot better.

Buzz Words and the Power of Language

So what are some of the key words you can use to help in your job hunt?

- Anything action oriented, if you're going to use a verb, make it active not passive wherever possible
- Formulated
- Generated
- Increased especially when flowed by a specific example
- Presented
- Programmed
- Analytical
- Bilingual and/or diplomatic (if you claim to be bilingual be prepared to back it up) and know that most posts seeking bilingual applicants require some degree of fluency
- Driven
- Flexible
- Evaluated
- Identified

Most job boards will have blogs and articles about current buzz words. One of the most extensive lists of words that also includes a breakdown of ones suited for particular fields is maintained by the Wisconsin Job Center (wisconsinjobcenter.org). It's good to look at these picking the ones that work for you (like a Vegas buffet), just make sure that you don't randomly drop buzz words into your resume and cover letter or your apt to end up with phrases like "I provided motivated support to multiple computer programs".

A good way to find good buzz words is to look at job postings. Look at the job you are applying for and see what words and language they use in the posting. Pick out a few keys ones and drop them into your cover letter.

Just as there are words that can help, there are also words that can hurt your job hunt and make your resume look weak. Many of these words by themselves aren't that bad, it's more that they're overused and not backed up with specific examples. Common toxic terms include:

- Enhanced
- Familiar with
- Solutions-oriented or Results-oriented
- Out-of-the-box or Creative
- Innovative
- Proven track record
- Motivated
- Team player
- Faced-paced
- Entrepreneurial
- Problem solver
- Interpersonal
- Communication skills

A quick Internet search will reveal lists of words and phrases to be avoided, and these lists are constantly being revised. Buzz words go in cycles just like job listings. All the more reason to dust off your resume and give it a review if you haven't had to look at for a few years. It's a good idea to vary the buzz words that you use. If you use "innovative" every single time on your application it loses its effect. Your application ends up sounding dry, canned, and dull. Not the dynamic impression you were hoping for. One final note about buzz words: there is such a thing as too much. Every sentence does not have to have buzz words, overuse of buzz words is wordy, awkward, and makes your application difficult to read.

9
SITES TO KNOW, SITES TO IGNORE

It has reached the point where asking how many job search sites are on the Internet is like asking how many grains of sand are on the beach. Pages and pages of job search engines can be overwhelming. The good news is that you don't need to search every single site every single day in order to be effective. In fact many career coaches agree that attempting to do so is actually counterproductive and a waste of your time. Instead it's not a matter of looking harder but of looking smarter. Put another way, if you search enough sites you'll start to notice that you'll see the same postings over and over again. No you're not losing your mind, cross-posting is rampant on search sites. Knowing that before you start will save you time and stress in the long run.

The websites below are a representative cross-section of what's available. This list by no means includes every single search engine that is available. In addition these are only sites that list positions from multiple companies. If there is a specific company that you really want to work for the best your best advice is to go directly to that company's website.

General Job Hunting Websites

Craigslist

Started in 1995 Craigslist was originally a way for people in San Francisco to share information about local events. Since then Craigslist has grown to be one of the largest 'post anything here' sites. It can be a good way to pick up short-term assignments (in the 'gigs' section) as well as regular job (in the 'jobs' section). However since anyone can post pretty much anything Craigslist has also become a haven for scammers, phishers, and pretty much any creep you can think of. Be extremely careful of what information you give out, be careful whom you meet and when, and any creative work you've created before you make it public (stealing people's work is one of the more benign problems of Craigslist). In addition people who post jobs on Craigslist often quote salaries well below the market norm. You may find yourself working for little or nothing ("unpaid internships" abound, many of them illegal).

Flex Jobs

Looking for a non-traditional work environment? Want a flex-time job or part-time job? Over 50 and still want to remain active in the workforce? Do you want to be a stay-at-home parent? If you answered yes to any of these questions than Flex Job is the site for you. Flex Job specializes in the entire etc. jobs that traditional job sites overlook.

Glassdoor

Glassdoor was co-founded in 2007 by Robert Hohman while he was taking time off from another search engine Hotwire. The concept was simple, to let employees (past and present) anonymously rate their employers including giving salary ranges for the various positions. With that Glassdoor provided a glimpse into the previously mysterious HR departments of various companies. It has also grown to include a section where people who have interviewed at a company can share notes about what their interview was like.

Glassdoor has an extensive collection of job postings. That can be narrowed down in a number of ways. However there are two things to note about Glassdoor: one is that there is no easy way to sort the results by the date posted so if you visit the site several times throughout the day it can be hard to determine if you are looking at new postings or existing postings. Two: reposting is rampant on this site. It is not uncommon to see the same jobs posted multiple times. This can make it difficult to figure of out if the job you are interested in is one that you looked at two pages back or not.

Indeed

Indeed is the #1 job site is the world (as of printing) reaching more than 50 countries. Like many other general search sites indeed gathers posts from other websites as well as listing jobs unique to Indeed. One of the best parts about Indeed is its search feature. Along with the usual options indeed allows you to narrow your search by salary. A word of caution about the salary search is that this depends on what the company listing put down as the salary. Many companies don't list a salary and therefore may be excluded from your search, and there is nothing to prevent a company from listing an incorrect salary. Outside of that Indeed allows you to narrow the time frame so that you search only for postings that are new "since your last visit". This is great if you visit the site several times in one day, you know that you're only getting new posts (although some will inevitably be reposts since nothing prevents a company from spamming their job post everywhere.

LinkedIn

LinkedIn is much more than a listing of available jobs, instead it aims to be the one-stop site for everything career related. The best features of LinkedIn are the various networking tools. LinkedIn is focused around the profile you create. Allow several hours to create your profile, and plan on doing weekly maintenance on it. Since your profile is what everything is based on LinkedIn is a site where you only get out of it what you put into it. Once you've created your profile you have access to a number of different tools (the site will try to upsell you on various services and features, but since I have not personally tested them I don't feel qualified to review them. I can say that I know a number of people who have used LinkedIn quite successfully without buying all the add-ons.). This is where LinkedIn really shines (and gets its name).

Networking is the name of the game. As you fill out your profile the site will suggest people that you might know ("You worked at XYZ Flowers and so did Mary, do you know each other?"), and suggest that you make a connection with them. If you agree the site makes the introductions and you two are connected. Connections are also grouped by degree (if you think of the Six Degrees of Kevin Bacon game you'll get the idea). Who should this matter? Because more and more people get their jobs through connections. Knowing people who work where you want to work is a terrific in. In addition LinkedIn is wonderful for people who are shy. While an online connection doesn't fully take the place of an in-person connection it is a great place to start.

A final benefit of LinkedIn is that you can make your profile viewable to the public with a unique website address. You can put this address on your cover letters allowing potential employers access to a more in-depth look at you including a portfolio of your work.

Monster

Considered one of the top five websites by many career counselors, Monster started their online recruitment presence in 1994 and since then has grown to include not only job postings, but career advice, and an array of services to help job seekers. Monster allows you to narrow your search by a number of factors to help pinpoint jobs that are of interest to you. In addition Monster makes it easy to apply to jobs and save resumes. Like many other sites Monster will offer to send you customized job updates to your email, while this is a convenient feature these job alerts can quickly clog your inbox.

The Ladders

The Ladders is a job site specifically for $100,000+ job seekers. Before you go thinking that you'll wander among the elite like and act like a party crasher at a country club, know that you will be asked for your most recent salary (and saying that you made $150,000 as a store checker will not fly). The site is considered tops among elite job hunters. They have recently expanded downward to include $80,000+ professionals, but I wouldn't count on them moving into the $30,000 and below any time soon.

Industry Specific Websites

Creative & Entertainment

Creative HotList

Although Creative HotList posts jobs of all types for creative professionals their main focus is on advertising.

Mandy.com

This site gives a good survey of available entertainment jobs. Most of these will be in the lo/no/deferred category, which means you'll end up with a credit on your resume and not much else. Still if you're looking to pick up a small gig this is a good place to check out.

MediaBistro

Any professional serious about their career should check out MediaBistro, which has become a large website with postings covering the entire creative spectrum. In addition MediaBistro has well-developed searched functions as well as offering articles and advice for creative professionals. Another facet of MediaBistro is that they offer courses to help creative professionals gain new skills and become more competitive and marketable.

TalentZoo

One thing sets TalentZoo apart from the other websites in this category, true they offer a well-developed list of jobs and the ability to create an account to make applying jobs easier, but they also offer a salary monitor. You can put in your location and industry in order to find out what the average salaries are in your area. This helps you to know if a potential employer is low-balling salaries and give you a more realistic idea of how much you can expect to make.

Education

Chronicle of Higher Education

While this site offers a large number of job postings for higher education professionals but the organization (or lack thereof) can make searching through the postings time-consuming.

HigherEd Jobs

HigherEd Jobs has a reputation as being one of the most comprehensive job boards for teachers and professors looking to get involved in teaching online. In addition this site offers many traditional teaching positions with a focus on teaching in higher education (university level).

SchoolSpring

Mainly focusing on non-post-secondary education, SchoolSpring is a large (and free) resource for teachers. Since this job board is nationwide as well as international it can be very useful if you are looking into relocating.

Financial

eFinancialCareers

One of the benefits of this very large job board is that it breaks down the postings by the specific type of financial professional being sought. If you deal in investment banking exclusively you don't have to wade through pages of posts for real estate and tax professionals.

In addition there is a special section aimed at internships and professionals new to the field.

Government
Federal
ClearanceJobs.com

This job board is exclusively for job seekers who currently possess some form of government security clearance. You need to already possess it in order to apply for these jobs (not just be eligible), and be able to prove it when you apply (employers will check). If you have a security clearance look here because it's something that will set you apart from other job seekers.

usajobs.gov

This is the official jobs website for the US Federal Government. To the point that you should be wary of other sites claiming to post federal government jobs (if they ask for any money, run and run fast). This site offers a mind-boggling number of ways to search for a job. Your first stop will be to create a profile something which takes almost an hour. If you have transcripts, supporting documentation, and any records or prior government or military service have then scanned (as separate files, not one big file) and ready to upload.

Once you have done that you are ready to search. I personally find that the best way to order the results is by Closing Date. This allows you to see what jobs are closing first and concentrate your efforts on those. The job descriptions are insanely detailed and complex so make sure you read every part of them. If you submit for a job most of the time you will also be taken to that specific department's site in order to complete additional information.

Although this is the go-to site for federal government jobs remember that these are federal government jobs the process takes forever. You have to be patient.

State and Local

To access these you'll have to search for (insert state name) government jobs and look for the official website. This can easily be confused with the website that the state will operate for local businesses looking to hire workers. Most states hire workers based on the results of specific examinations. Not only will you have find an open position (one that isn't an internal hire only), but you also have to make sure that you can take the required examinations in time (as these examinations are only given a few times a year and not on a regular schedule this can be a logistical nightmare). Good news is that once you take the examinations your scores are good for other jobs of that type (as long as it's listed).

Health & Medicine

HealthECareers

HealthECareers and Medhunters merged under the umbrella of HealthECareers which maintains a large database of jobs not only for doctors and nurses but for a wide array of other health professionals (dentists, medical imaging, pharmacy, etc.). You are also offered a wide variety of options to narrow down your search and several different ways to display the results (including by date). One of the best features is that medical professionals can also specify a specialty, making it useful (no wading through posts for pediatricians to find the posts for anesthesiologists).

MD Jobsite

This is a site that specializes in just what its name says, medical doctors. Although they will list jobs for other specialties if you belong to another medical specialty devoting large amounts of time to this site might not be a wise investment.

Medzilla

Although Medzilla offers listings for medical professionals its real strength lies in postings for pharmaceutical professionals as well as those in the biotech and medical research fields. The layout of this site is very busy and can be intimidating, but it's worth wading through the noise to find a solid and well-stocked job board.

Hospitality
careersinfood.com

If your job has to do with food, food production, distribution or anything else food related than this site is worth checking out. At any given time this site has over 13,000 jobs posted. Worried that all these jobs are only for fast food? think again. These jobs cover every aspect and level of anything having to do with food production and distribution.

hcareers.com

Want to search beyond the traditional hotel or country club than this site is for you. While hcareers.com offers plenty of traditional hotel and country club jobs you'll also be able to tap into the more diverse side of hospitality including cruise ships, casinos, theme parks and more. In addition a clean and easy to navigate interface makes job hunting almost enjoyable.

hospitalityonline.com

On any given day hospitalityonline.com has over 10,000 jobs aimed at hospitality professionals available. This site also offers postings for museums and since employers have to pay in order to post jobs the chance that you'll be applying for dummy jobs (ones that don't exist) is reduced.

hoteljobs.com

As with many other job boards you can post your resume on hoteljobs.com and preform all of the usual job searches. One thing that sets this site apart is its uncluttered layout which easily allows you to find the information you are looking for. In addition this site focuses on exactly what its name implies, hotel careers

Law

Find Law

Fresh out of law school or looking for a job and need not only job listings, access to legal resources, then Find Law is your site. In addition this site allows you to narrow your search by specialty and provides a section for jobs focused specifically at interns. Although this site is free be prepared to cope with lots of ads and a very cluttered page. Still worth it in the long run.

lawjobs.com

Run by ALM, lawjobs.com specializes in not only legal but also real estate jobs. Although ALM (in its current incarnation) has only been around since 2012, ALM has been around for over a century under different names. ALM maintains job postings around the entire country, but with most of their offices located on the East coast that is where their real strength lies.

Martindale-Hubbell Legal Careers

This site serves everyone from law students just starting out to seasoned professionals. In addition job seekers take advantage of such features as a salary survey, access to recruiters and career advice aimed at legal professionals.

Manufacturing

manufacturingjobs.com

In addition to offering a large number of manufacturing and production jobs at this site you can set up job alerts, post your resume, and narrow your search using a number of different parameters. One of the nicest aspects of this site is that even though it's a free site it is very clean and well laid out with a minimal number of ads and other distracting clutter.

Non-Profit

Idealist

Want to make a difference as well as a paycheck? Idealist is the site for you. Many of the jobs listed are from non-profits and they are looking for all different types of employees. One thing to note is that in addition to paying jobs idealist also posts volunteer jobs, make sure you know which one you're looking it before you apply. Idealist is free and in addition to the job board you'll have access to a wide range of blog posts and articles. It's worth looking at them to find ways to tailor to your application to the non-profit job market.

Retail

allretailjobs.com

One of the largest job boards dedicated to retail workers, allretailjobs.com offers many different ways to search for jobs. You can register and create an account which allows you to apply for jobs quickly. In addition they offer a variety of resume services (for a fee). Although you'll have thousands of posts at your fingertips the layout of the site is cluttered so be prepared to spend some time learning to navigate your way around.

jobs.nrf.com

Work in retail and never heard of the NRF? Don't worry you're not alone, the NRF is the National Retail Federation. Most major retailers belong to this organization which recently launched their own job board for retail workers. Since this is such a new site your search options are limited and there are not the massive numbers of posts that other sites offer, still what posts are here are quality posts usually focused more on retail management and corporate jobs.

workinretail.com

Whereas the National Retail Federation job board is focused more on retail and corporate management workinretail.com focuses more on sales associates and in-store retail employees. A nice feature of this site is that you can narrow down what type of retail job you want to work. Have experience as a barista? This site allows you to search only for barista jobs. Only want to search by the most recent or closest jobs? Workinretail.com lets you do that.

Sales & Marketing

SalesJobs.com

This site does just want the name implies. It lists sales jobs and only sales jobs. With a large searchable database there is pretty much any type of sales job you could imagine. In addition SalesJobs.com offers all of the usual resume posting and job alerts.

VentureBeat.com

Not only is this the go-to site that recruiters go to in order to advertise their sales and marketing jobs, but this site has gained a reputation as the site to go to for specialty sales and marketing jobs. Things like pharmaceutical sales and inside sales find their home here. If you have a unique sales niche that sets you apart look here for matching jobs. Does it matter if you have a niche? Yes. There might be fewer jobs for your niche, but you can fill them (and they'll likely pay more).

Science & Technology

Aerotek

Founded in 1983 Aerotek is a staffing agency (meaning that companies list their jobs with Aerotek and Aerotek lists them on their site and is responsible for gathering all the application paperwork). Aerotek specializes in technology, biotechnology, scientific manufacturing, as well as A- aerotech and some pharmaceutical. Basically if your job has to do with science and engineering than Aerotek should be near the top of your places to look. The only drawback to Aerotek is its organization. Looking for jobs and filtering them is not intuitive and even after performing searches several times it is still easy to get lost.

Careers2.0

A massive job board aimed at technology professionals careers2.0 matches recruiters and marketers to you, the job seeker. In this massive site it is easy to get lost among everyone else so make sure to spruce up your resume and find ways to set yourself apart from all the other job seekers on the site (so you know UNIX, we have a thousand people that can do that, what else can you do?)

CyberCoders

CyberCoders posts jobs for everything computer and technology related. Its real niche is in computer programming, but more recently has branched out to include, tech repair and graphic design jobs. Jobs posted on this site are looking for people who are experts in their particular programming language and this usually means having the certifications to back it up.

Dice.com

Dice is one of the most comprehensive job boards for tech professionals. In addition to a large number of jobs (which is the most important part of a job board), Dice offers blogs, resume services (for a fee), and a host of other benefits. Searching Dice is also easy and you can narrow your results by a number of different factors including salary. Dice is almost everything you'd want in a job board, but one thing to watch out for is that you read all of the options especially anything with a check box next to it or you'll find your inbox flooded with email.

Thoughts on Pay Websites

The websites I have listed are all free (although many will offer you additional services for a fee) this is because while you're job hunting you don't have extra money to throw around. There are a number of job boards that charge a membership fee, but I would be wary of such sites. I have never heard of someone who actually did pay and that made the difference in landing the job. Be wary of sites that ask for money because they might just simply repost jobs that are available for free elsewhere. Your money could be better spent maintaining membership (and connections) in professional organizations which allows you an in with corporations in your field.

A Final Thought (or Two)

This is by no means a complete listing of job boards and as you progress through your job hunt you'll add to this list with your own. You'll find hidden gems of sites and a lot of sites that waste your time. Instead this chapter is intended to give you a starting off point, a base from which to depart. Keep track of what sites work for you to refer to, keep a list of what sites are a waste of time so you know not to return to them. In addition just because a job is listed in one category does not mean that you won't find jobs listed that are for another category. Many recruiters are swamped and indiscriminately blast out a job announcement to every job board they can find without stopping to see where they are posting.

The most important thing is to develop a system that works for you and stick with it. Since I search through several different sites every day I have a Bookmarks folder on my browser that has all of them bookmarked. Not only do I save in typing in the addresses each time, but with all of them listed I can go right down the list one after another and that way I am sure that I've checked every one. Again it's a whatever works for you policy.

10
BY THE NUMBERS

Job hunting runs on numbers. After all how else are you to judge how well you're doing? It all comes down to numbers, or does it? It's easy to get caught up in the endless statistics forgetting the quote "There's lies, damned lies and statistics". The truth is that while statistics are interesting they don't speak directly to you as a unique individual. How is it that statistics can be useful and useless at the same time?

Take the statistic (that I made up) that the average person will look for a job for six months before getting an offer. First of all this is an average meaning that for some people it will be less (one month? one week?). second of all our average is said about the getting of a job offer. Nothing is said about the quality of this offer. If you get an offer but it's at one-half your former salary, none of your benefits, twice the hours, and something you hate doing, it that really a good offer? There's actually an economic term for this type of downward movement, underemployment. Just because you're given an offer does not mean you automatically should accept it. There is such a thing as an offer you should refuse.

So Where Does That Leave Us?

According to the first quarter of 2013 Employment Confidence Survey released by the job information networking site Glassdoor (http://www.glassdoor.com) "Younger employees are more confident about finding a job six months after being laid off than their older counterparts." While this is interesting, the takeaway message is that no matter your age confidence is an essential part of your job hunt. If you don't believe in yourself and your ability to do the job, it will be very hard to convince an interviewer that you can. It's how you gain confidence that's the tricky part. A manager once told me that my biggest problem was confidence. "You're not confident enough. You need to be more confident." If anyone's ever told you this it becomes even harder to gain confidence. Still confidence is essential even if you start out by faking it.

What's the Difference Between a Separation and a Layoff Event?

"It's a lay off when your neighbor loses their job. It's a recession when you lose yours."

When it comes to Bureau of Labor Statistics a separation is when you get laid off. A layoff event is when fifty (or more) employees at a company are laid off. An important note is that the Bureau of Labor Statistics generally reports only this level of detail. The reasons why people have been separated of laid off is buried further into the report and is generally broken down into seven categories:

1. Business Demand: An easy way to think of this is if you work at a shop making computers the size of rooms and a state-of-the-art laptop computer comes on the market. Demand for your now antiquated computer will plummet. Less demand equals less revenue equals less ability to pay employees. Many times this is the number one cause of employees losing their jobs.
2. Organizational Changes: One common way to think of this is that new management is brought in and the department

(or company) is reorganized. This is especially true if your job is duplicated, or made redundant.
3. Financial Issues: These are any job losses due to bankruptcy, pressure for more profits, or other measures designed to try and save a failing company or make a company more profitable.
4. Production Specific: This is mainly tied to the manufacturing industry. If the assembly line is fully automated there will be a decreased demand for assembly line workers. In addition if a factory is unable (due to natural or manmade disasters) to obtain the raw materials needed for production than the assembly line will slow down. Lower production equals lower profits results less money to pay employees.
5. Disaster/Safety: Any condition that makes working difficult or hazardous affects a company's ability to pay workers.
6. Seasonal: The most common way to think of this are holiday sales employees. They are hired in late October to work the holiday shopping season and are laid off on January at the end of the holiday shopping season. Other popular seasons are the summer recreational and landscaping seasons.
7. Other/Miscellaneous: This category is for everything that doesn't fit into the other categories.

Why Does This Matter?

You'll notice that no specific numbers have been placed beside the different categories. That's because the specific numbers don't matter. What matters is that a whole lot of people lose their jobs over circumstances entirely beyond their control. So find out what was beyond your control and ignore it. Find out what was within your control and work to change it.

A Sobering Number…to Ignore.

In unemployment circles a common statistic cited is the number of people looking for a job versus the number of jobs actually available. It's usually cites as "3.7 million people are still fighting for every single available job". A quick read of that statement might scare you to death, and in a way it's designed to do just that. First of all fighting for a job has much more emotional impact that looking for a job (which is what most people do). In addition this statistic is for the entire United States, unemployment rates change not only from state to state but also city to city. Finally, I would venture to guarantee that not all those 3.7 million people are looking for and applying for the same jobs as you.

The Most Important Number in Job Hunting
One.
- Your focus should be on your job hunt. What everyone else, and what some statistic says about everyone else doesn't really matter. Your focus is on doing what you can to get yourself a job.
- The minimum number of job offers required to get you a job. You don't need a dozen offers, you're not going to be working a dozen places. At its simplest you need a job offer that you accept to have a job.

11
THE JOB HUNTING YEAR

Just as the average work week runs on a schedule, so does the job hunting world. In the working world it's common knowledge that the worst time to schedule a meeting is on a Friday before a holiday weekend right after lunch (unless you're purposefully trying to hide a meeting, then it's perfect). The same goes for the world of job hunting. Jobs are continually being posted, but knowing a bit about the schedules can help you plan for and better understand why your job hunt goes the way it does.

Job Hunting Throughout the Year:

1. January-March:
    a. Pros: For many companies the new year means new budgets. If they have extra cash they may be in the hiring mood.
    b. Cons: Seasonal employees will be re-entering the market. Just because they worked a holiday/seasonal job doesn't mean that they don't have the skills to compete.

2. April-June:
    a. Pros: Companies gear up hiring in anticipation of flood of new graduates applying.
    b. Cons: You'll be competing against graduates whose diploma's still have wet ink. Your advantage? Experience! You have real world experience so play it up, and be creative. Look beyond your job descriptions, in most jobs you'll find yourself doing tasks you weren't hired to do. That's valuable experience.
3. July-September:
    a. Pros: Jobs are still posted! Look to education which is staffing up now. In addition many people take the summer off believing that companies don't post jobs now. Keep at it and your perseverance may be rewarded.
    b. Cons: While jobs are posted and people are hired, everything seems to work in slow motion. It takes longer for anything to happen and making contact with anyone can be an agonizing game of phone tag.
4. October-December:
    a. Pros: October is the rush time for seasonal employment. Don't knock it, you can get some extra cash, merchandise discounts, and perhaps the chance to stay on long-term and move up (although this last incentive is dangled in front of all seasonal employees, on average for every 30 seasonal employees there are only 2-3 'regular' jobs actually available). Proactive hiring managers will want to hire now in order to have someone on-board and ready for the new year.
    b. Cons: The holidays. Avoid sending out resumes from shortly before Thanksgiving until after the New Year. People will be on vacation and otherwise occupied meaning your carefully crafted application is likely to

get lost at the bottom of an inbox. In addition getting in contact with anyone will be almost impossible. Instead use this time to network (holiday parties can be great) and get rest so you can hit the pavement running.

The Job-Hunting Week

While jobs are posted every day there exists a rhythm to the job-hunting week. Knowing this rhythm can help you plan for maximum results.

Monday:
- Avoid Interviews. It's hard to hold people's attention when they're still thinking about the weekend.

Tuesday:
- Best Day to Interview!

Wednesday:
- Most Jobs Posted. Boards are alive with posts so be prepared to do lots of applications. Check back throughout the day for new posts.
- Most Applications Reviewed. This is when the hiring managers kick into high gear.
- Best Day to Interview!

Thursday:
- Best Day to Interview!
- Monitor Applications Sent Today. If the job postings don't close until next Wednesday and you submit today you might end up at the bottom of the pile.

Friday:
- Avoid Interviews. People are only thinking about the weekend, they could care less about you.
- Preferred Firing Day.

The Best Time

Although there is still some debate many believe that the time of day you interview can have an impact on your chances of getting the job. In general the best times to interview are between 9am-11am and again between 2pm-4pm. If you can interview between these times Tuesday-Thursday you stand the best chance of having the full attention of the interviewer and being able to make the best impression.

Unfortunately you may not be given the chance to pick your day and time, especially if several interviewers schedules are being coordinated. If not graciously accept the time offered and make the best of it.

The Offer Timeline

Even though it's wonderful to fanaticize that you are offered the position on the spot this rarely happens. Instead count on waiting between a week and ten days before hearing something after an interview. Send your thank you note immediately after the interview and continue on life as normal. Don't call every day and bug them. If you haven't heard back in about two weeks you might consider a discrete follow-up inquiry. If you find out you didn't get the position thank them, ask them to keep you in mind for future positions, and above all do not beg for the job and harass them to tell you why you weren't hired.

12
THE EMOTIONAL ROLLERCOASTER

Job hunting is an emotional rollercoaster. Long periods of boredom, depression and nothing punctuated by brief moments of anticipation, anxiety and excitement followed by even more anxiety and anticipation often ending with an emotional catharsis (either positive or negative). How can you survive this?

The Job Hunting Lifecycle

Understanding that job hunting follows a basic three stage lifecycle can make things more bearable.

1. The Rush. This is the first stage of your job hunt. You're sending out lots of resumes and not hearing any response. You haven't done anything wrong it's just too soon to hear back. Jobs in government and academia are typically posted for weeks. During this time no one looks at the applications they just gather in a big electronic mailbox. Even in private industry it can take weeks before someone gets around to looking at them. In this stage no news is good news because it means you're still in the running.

2. The Dump. This is the hardest stage because this is when employers send out rejections to people they won't even

interview. Seeing one generic rejection after another pile up in your inbox is difficult. Just cross them off the list and file the notices away. It seems like this stage lasts forever, but in reality it will end.
3. The Reward. At this stage you'll start to receive requests for interviews. This can take a long time. In government and academia it's not unheard of to submit for a job and not be contacted for an interview until 4+ months later (my personal record is being asked to interview eight months after I had applied).

It is important to remember that you need to keep looking and applying throughout this entire cycle. You just have to keep at it even when it seems hopeless.

Combating Anxiety and Shyness

You look great on paper and you have an awesome cover letter. Unfortunately employees are rarely hired based on their applications alone. Interviews are the crucible in which applicants are judged. Great news if you're a natural born salesperson of yourself, but if you're like the majority of job hunters thoughts of interviews bring up your anxiety and shyness. You have to master these emotions if you want to get a job.
1. Deodorant. It sounds obvious, but when you get anxious you sweat. Sweat shows, sweat smells, and does not make a good impression. If you're someone who sweats a lot stash some deodorant in your car and do one last application before you walk in. Think your sweat will show or that it has? Keep your jacket on and your arms down. If you're driving to the interview you can wear a t-shirt in the car and do a quick change before you go in (this works well in the summer or hot climates).
2. Be Comfortable. You're in an uncomfortable situation so try to make your clothes as comfortable as possible. This is not

the place to try out those new dress shoes. Wear clothes that fit (your interviewer will not care that you squeezed into a size 8 instead of a 12) and are as comfortable as interview clothes can be. Wear tennis shoes or sandals and change into your dress shoes beforehand.

3. Be Early. If you're not out of breath and rushing you'll have time to compose yourself.
4. Frame and Reframe. By giving a context and reframing things you'll give the interviewer a picture beyond your application. One common example of this is a thin resume without much experience. Reframe a question about lack of experience to highlight other work you have done. Part of keeping anxiety in check is not just thinking of questions, but also thinking of answers. You don't have control over the questions but you do have control over the answers.
5. Acknowledge the Elephant. The elephant in this case is your anxiety. There's a decent chance that your interviewer will notice your anxiety especially if it's severe. Left unacknowledged it may lead the interviewer to think that you won't be able to handle the stresses of the job. One of the best ways to deal with this is to confront it head-on. Acknowledge your anxiety, comment about how it is due to your excitement for the position, and make a statement about how it won't affect your job performance. Be positive and proactive. At some point the interviewer was in your chair. Keep that in mind.
6. Don't Apologize. Be positive about who you are. This is not the place to sell yourself short or put qualifiers behind your statements. In an interview fake it 'til you make it is the mantra. Remember that interviews by their nature are short (usually 30 minutes to an hour). Even the worst interview will end, it will give you a great story and leave you with experience you can take to the next interview.
7. Concentrate on You. This interview is about you. Don't get

caught up trying to size up the other candidates (easily done in a group interview or if you're sitting together in the waiting room). Concentrate on doing the best you can, ultimately you are the only person you can control.
8. Make the Interview Work for You. Many introverts and shy people excel at one-on-one communication, make this work for you. While extremely extroverted and social people may have difficulty in one-on-one this is your strength, make it work.
9. Make the Most of Online. In-person networking events scare you? Maximize online social networking sites. You'll get the benefits of social networking, but in an environment that's more comfortable.
10. Plan Your Day. The day of your interview careful planning can help keep your anxiety at bay. Try not to plan anything before your interview. Don't do any job hunting beforehand. After the interview plan a calm and relaxing activity. Make sure to eat and drink well. It can be helpful to imagine your interview suit as a suit of armor that protects you and allows you to go confidently into the interview.

Types of Interviews

There are a few basic types of interview and knowing which one you're walking into can help you deal effectively with them.

1. One-on-One. This is the most common type. It consists of you and the interviewer. Pros: Only one person you have to make a connection with and direct your answers to. Cons: If they don't like you that's it.
2. One-on-Many. This consists of you interviewing with a panel of interviewers (2-5 seems to be the norm). Pros: Your success is not determined by one person. Cons: You have to successfully connect with every single interviewer and somehow remember everyone's name.

3. Many-on-One and Many-on-Many. These are generally the most confusing and stressful types of interviews. It's a group of candidates in a room with one or more interviewers. This reminds me of a reality show where all the candidates in the room are competing for the prize in this case a job. Pros: (I can't think of any). Cons: You have to fight it out with other candidates to emerge on top while gaining the notice (in a positive way) of the interviewers.

4. The Remote (Phone or Internet): It can involve any combination of people interviewing you. This is most commonly done when you live some distance from your prospective employer. It can also be done as a very, very quick screener to see if they want to see you in the flesh. Pros: If it's over the phone and there is no video component you don't have to dress up (you could do it in the buff if you really want) and you can have notes in front of you to refer to. While this doesn't take the place of preparation it can take some of the stress off. Cons: That damned technology! Dropped calls, scrambled video feeds, and software incompatibility can make this a nightmare. In addition there is the missing element, you're never going to get quite the same interaction and connection as an in-person interview. In addition since so much communication is non-verbal you'll miss out on important cues (beware of any type of humor!) and they'll miss out on knowing you as a real live person.

13
DEALING WITH REJECTION

A large part of any job hunt is rejection. Rejection comes in many forms and at many stages. In the first stage your application is rejected right away. Once you're interviewed you'll likely experience a second type if rejection. Each of these types of rejection has a unique characteristics and unique ways of handling them.

Stage One Rejection

You fill out the application and submit your resume. You're happy because you're perfect for the job. It's a sure thing, until you receive the working world's equivalent of a 'Dear John' letter. What happened?

Look at what you put on the application, not your resume, but the fill in the blank form you submitted. Many Human Resources departments overwhelmed by the massive volume of applications they receive, employ job bots. Job bots are computer programs that search through applications looking for key words/phrases that will allow the program to automatically reject or accept the application. While these programs are designed to make the job of Human Resources easier, they create a nightmare for job seekers. If you don't have the right combination of buzz words and phrases (or have the wrong ones), for the job the job bot will automatically reject your application. If you're getting rejections for jobs you're qualified for reexamine what you're putting down on the application. Try to use the same wording that the job posting and job description uses. Chances are the job bot is keyed to look for the same phrases that are in the job posting.

At this stage don't let rejection get to you. Take the e-mail or letter, cross the job off of your submission log and file the letters away. Don't throw the letters out in case someone from the Unemployment Bureau wants to see proof of your job hunt. Beyond that don't take it personally, it's all part of the process.

Stage Two Rejection

At this stage the rejection becomes much more personal and emotional. To get ready for an interview you have to psych yourself up, building up the reasons you want the job and the reasons you are perfect for the job. You're on this high which makes the crash of rejection all the worse. It's easy to take it personally because in many respects it can be. So what do you do?

Contact the person who interviewed you. Be nice and polite. Ask them why, but don't question their answer and don't be surprised if they can't/won't give you an answer. Quickly move on to the real point of your call (or note), thank them for their time, express your continued interest in the company and enthusiastically ask if they will keep you in mind for any future jobs they might have. Turn them into a contact, a relationship that you should nurture because it may pay off in the future.

But what about your feelings? All that hurt, anger and frustration is eating you alive. Talk to friends, family anyone that is not related to the company that just rejected you. Cry about it, have a pint of ice cream, get the emotions out. Don't suppress your feelings. If you don't get these feelings through your system they will hinder your future job hunt. You'll stare at your computer unmotivated and apathetic about applying for jobs. In future interviews your negative feelings and thoughts will be hard to ignore making you seem distracted and distant (at the worst you'll present as hostile). Get it out now, it'll be better in the long run. Once you've done this you can move on to the next steps.

Now comes the hard part, an honest examination of what went wrong. This is not fun but it is essential so that you don't repeat the same mistakes. Some things are easy to change, others may take more work.

On the easy to correct side: were you on time, polite to everyone and dressed appropriately? Appearances are other little things matter. What was your attitude? You have to be enthusiastic and positive during an interview. Interviewers don't care about your personal problems. If you aren't positive your negative attitude will pervade the interview and poison your chances. Were you prepared? A little knowledge goes a long way. Know the company (and position) you're interviewing for. It shows that you actually want the job.

A strong ending is key. If you hung your head, gave a limp handshake and mumbled your good byes your interviewer will be left with the impression you don't want or care about the job. Instead give a firm handshake, make eye contact, enthusiastically thank the interviewer and ask for the job. If you want the job, ask for it!

Want to create a great impression? Write a thank you note. You get another chance to make a positive impression and it's one of the classiest things you can do.

In Closing

Even if you do everything right you still may not get the job. Things happen that are beyond your control (or knowledge). What's important is that you pick yourself up and get back out there. Job offers won't drop in your lap you have to work for them. Learn from your mistakes and move on. In the end you are not judged by how many times you fail, but by if you rise in the end.

14
GOING BACK

Yes, people do go back and work for the same company that let them go. Although it can be a positive thing it's a potential minefield that must be traversed with caution. Some important points to consider before jumping back into your old role.
1. Why did you leave (or were asked to leave) in the first place: If you and your boss hated each other before chances are you'll hate each other the second time around. On the other hand if you were let go due to an economic downturn going back may not be so bad.
2. How was your exit: If your exit the first time around was remembered for the yelling, shouting, things being thrown and police being called, it's a pretty sure bet you're not going to be rehired. On the other hand if you managed to remain civil and professional, you might have a chance. Last impressions can matter as much as first impressions.
3. Where will you be: Working in the exact same department for the exact same boss will be a lot more difficult than working for a different

department for a different boss in a large organization.
4. What was the official reason for your leaving:
Even if Human Resources lists your reason for leaving as "Poor Performance" office gossip can carry a huge amount of weight. So if gossip says your real reason for leaving was you "pissed off every coworker and messed up everything you touched" that can have an impact on your chances of getting rehired. But all is not bad news. If you were a well-liked and productive employee who was a victim of situational issues (e.g. the impossible job, things beyond your control) positive gossip may help overcome a vague Human Resources reason for leaving.

Maximizing Your Chances of Rehire:
1. Don't Burn Your Bridges:
This starts before you're let go. Be nice to your coworkers, be the type of person they can depend on (and relate to). For shy people this can be difficult, but if other employees get to know you as more than a coworker (remembering to still maintain professionalism) it helps in the long run. Also remember that interested is interesting. Find out one thing that each of your coworkers (and definitely your boss) is interested in. Gain some knowledge about this so that you can talk about it. For shy people or if your coworker/boss is interested in something that is completely foreign to you this can be hard. (As a naturally artistic person talking the latest sports stats can be hard, just remember it's for a good cause… your job.)
2. Maintain Your Bridges:
Sometimes it seems coffee shops were made for this. When you leave your job it may be with bitter feelings, making reaching out to former coworkers especially hard. In addition you may feel awkward because these people are your friends but they are also a resource. You'll be asking

them for references. For this reason be the one to reach out with the invite, keep it professional, and buy the coffee.

3. Play Up Your Knowledge:
   Tailor your resume and application to showcase your expertise of your former (and hopefully future) employer. This does not mean dish on politics and people. If it was confidential when you worked there than pretend that you know nothing about it. If you're asked about a confidential project it's best to either claim no knowledge or simply state that you don't feel comfortable discussing such matters during an interview. Why? Because those are company secrets and there's no way of knowing if the person interviewing you actually knows what they're asking about or if they just picked up a bit of gossip at the water-cooler. In addition you'll win points for showing that you know better than to dish on company secrets. This is the place to mention your expertise in company or industry software, products, or policy. It shows that if hired you're ready to hit the ground running. Your employer won't have to spend as long showing you the basics.
4. Tailor Your Approach:
   You want to return with a positive and confident attitude. Don't return with your head hung with shame and your tail between your legs. Such a negative approach only sets you up for failure.
5. Be Prepared:
   You're still going to have to answer questions about why you left. Be prepared with an answer. Be positive in what you say. Be honest, your answer will be verified.
6. Network:
   Let people know you're interested in returning. Spread you're reach beyond your former department. You never know when a job in a different department will open up.

7. Be Professional:
    Even though you may know everyone in the company take the time and effort to be professional. Update you resume and cover letter. If you get an interview dress like you would for any other interview, even if you know your interviewers and know it's a causal work environment.

One final point. If you do return to work for a former employer be happy that they obviously see things in you that they like. Find out what they are and make them shine. Don't forget that they may also have seen things that they didn't like. Work on correcting them. Finally whatever you do don't dwell on the past. Look positively towards the future.

15
I WAS…

Scenario 1:
There you sit coffee mug on your table scrolling through job postings when you hit gold. The job posting written especially for you. Eagerly you upload your resume your fingers flying through the application until you stop dead taunted by the blinking cursor.

Scenario 2:
You're in the interview and it's going great. They like you. You like them. An offer is in the air, and then the interviewer says "One last question". You freeze and a stony silence hangs in the room.

What one question could cause such terror?
Why did you leave your previous job?
Or the even more terrifying, have you ever been fired of asked to leave a job and why?

What Can Your Previous Employer Say About You?
a. Your name and job title
b. The dates of your employment and your salary

c. A & B
   d. Anything they want

Answer: d. It's a popular myth that if asked your former can provide only the basics (name, job title, dates of employment, and salary). In fact there are no federal laws that restrict what your former employers can say. They can say how you left (fired, laid off, etc.) and they can provide the reason why. This is why it is essential that the reason you give for leaving matches your former employers' reason for letting you go. Any discrepancy between the two may be misconstrued as your lying on a job application/interview. You get caught doing that and any prospective employer can't shred your application fast enough. To make matters worse if you've applied for multiple positions with the same company you're likely to be barred from consideration from those as well.

Whatever you do don't lie! Spin the fact, polish the turd, but whatever you do don't lie!

That being said most former employers will not go into the dirty details of why you left. Why? They don't want to say anything that isn't strictly accurate or factual. If they do veer from the narrow path of accuracy and factuality and get caught (by you, which isn't likely) then they are subject to very large and very ugly libel and slander lawsuits.

So the less said the better on everyone's part.

What to Say?

You're going to be asked several times and in several ways to explain what happened. At this point consistency is key. Develop a short, 1-2 sentence statement about what happened. Rehearse this statement over and over so that when you are asked about your termination in an interview the answer rolls off your tongue and you deliver it calmly, without batting an eyelash, and with such confidence that any further questions on the matter evaporate from your interviewers mind. That level of confidence takes practice.

Things You Might Want to Say:
   A. Highlight your successes and achievements.
   B. As little as possible. This is not the time to wax poetically. Remember your goal is to answer as quickly as possible and move on to the next topic.
   C. If you were fired for something you specifically did/did not do turn it into a positive. Highlight how you've learned and grown from this experience.
   D. Admit responsibility. This one's tricky because it invites talking about your failure and before you know it you've fallen on your sword. This is never a pretty sight, especially in interviews.
   E. What about the impossible job? You could talk about the problems with the job and the unrealistic expectations, but be very careful because this could come across as playing the blame game.
   F. Anytime you can start your answer with the phrase "I learned…" you're on the right track.

What Not to Say:
   A. Under no circumstances lie!
   B. Do not mention any legal action or litigation with any former employer ongoing or settled. Any interviewer that hears legal, lawsuit, or litigation will panic wondering if you're a walking lawsuit just waiting to sue them.
   C. Do not badmouth, put down, or gossip about your former employer.
   D. Do not hint, joke about, or offer to share corporate secrets, or confidential information about your former employer. Any confidentiality and/or non-disclosure agreements you signed are still in effect even though you don't work for that company. In addition how can a future employer expect you to maintain confidentiality for them if you can't for a former

employer?

E. On applications and cover letters avoid mentioning being fired. If you have to give a reason write "will prefer to discuss in person". If that's too long go for "job ended". Avoid writing "fired" at all costs.

F. Do You Even Have to Mention the Job? Most of us have had that job we weren't at long enough to learn where the bathroom was. These clutter up your resume and make you look like a job hopper. Besides many applications limit how many previous jobs you can list. Make the space count and ditch the two day jobs.

Remember Your Audience

If you're interviewing for a different job with your former employer there are some addition considerations. Do not lie, this is even more important because office gossip and the fact that your future boss may know your former boss almost guarantee that you'll be caught in any lie. When Human Resources is literally down the hall it's a sure bet someone will ask. Use your knowledge of company policy as a selling point. If you come from a "problem department/division" this might work in your favor as you are seen as a casualty of the department's dysfunction. In this case do not bring up the dysfunction, if it's there than it's likely your interviewer already knows about it. If your interviewer comments on the troubled department give a short non-committal answer. Under no circumstances take this as an invitation to complain or dish on your former department.

If you are interviewing with a completely different company remember they may or may not know the inner workings and politics of your former employer. It doesn't matter. Your job is to simply answer the question and get on to the next topic.

Remember your job is to represent yourself in the most positive and truthful light, always remaining calm and professional. At one point your interviewer had to interview for their position and chances are good they had been fired once. We've all been there.

16
MISSION ACCOMPLISHED

Maybe you're peaking ahead seeing what lies at the end of the job hunting rainbow, or maybe you've exercised amazing self-control waiting until you have your offer letter in hand, but for whatever reason you've made it! Congratulations! Your hard work has paid off.

If the offer letter is made in person be happy but be professional. If you're alone when the good news comes now's the time to break out the celebratory dances and screaming. But why dedicate an entire chapter to celebrating job offers you may ask. Notice I've only said that you've received your job offer… you still have to accept it (or you could reject it).

If you've done your homework and research on the company you'll already have an idea if this is the type of place you'd like to work. If this is you're only offer letter and times are tough evaluate if you'd be taking this job as a stop gap and still continue looking. This is the point that all the intangibles of a job come into play.

If this is your only job offer: Consider how well this job meets your needs. Remember that there are more important things than salary. A high paying job doing something you hate of find morally repugnant may quickly lead to you losing your job of being fired and out of work again.

If you have two or more job offers: It's best to list out the pros and cons of each/all. Again there's more than salary to consider.

Negotiating for a better offer is always an option and there are shelves of books on how to negotiate effectively. Just remember that there is an element of risk associated with negotiating. You may end up overplaying your hand and end up losing the offer all together.

One important thing is that no book, article, or website can tell you if your job offer is a good one that you should accept. Only you (and your loved ones if they're involved) know what's best for you and your situation. Ultimately you're the one that is going to be doing the job day in and day out.

If this seems overwhelming just remember that you're making a commitment to a job, this is not a lifelong commitment. Most people change careers several times not to mention the number of jobs most people have. As great as this job seems chances are it won't be the only, or last, job that you will have. In the end it's only a job it's not a life sentence. If you hate it you can always get another, the fact that you just got this job is proof that you do indeed have the skills necessary to get a job.

The other rule of job offers: A handshake is great, a verbal offer is nice, but a firm signed offer letter is best. Unless it's in writing it's not official (and even then it's debatable).

Accepting An Offer: If you've decided to accept reply both verbally and in writing. Get a firm start date as well as any instructions about pre-employment paperwork (background check, etc.). Make sure you know who you report to and when. Write thank you letters to your interview committee and tell them how much you look forward to working with them.

Celebrate! Have a nice dinner and enjoy the feeling of accomplishment. Spread the good word and thank family and friends for their support. Chances are money is tight and will be until you get your first paycheck so be creative about celebrating on a budget.

What not to do? Anything that could possibly land you in legal trouble. This means no driving drunk, illegal drug use, and be careful what you post on the web and social media. Get caught doing this and you can kiss you're your job offer goodbye.

Get ready for your first day. Smile. Be confident. Be early. Remember this is your new job and first impressions matter. You've learned a lot about how strong and resourceful you are by job hunting, so you can do this. Leave the past in the past. Say as little as possible about your former employer, people will be curious. Stick to short positive statements, by now you've mastered your answer from doing interviews.

Above all... smile! They hired you because they saw potential in you so let it shine!

ABOUT THE AUTHOR

Jennifer B. Anderton is a writer, passionate about helping others find not only jobs, but jobs that will be fulfilling, believe that you should not live for a job, but have job so that you can live. She has bachelor degrees in English and Psychology as well as a Master of Arts degree in Marriage and Family therapy. Ms. Anderton also maintains an active blog about all things related to job hunting and maintaining a healthy work-life balance which can be found at: www.jenniferanderton.com.

www.ingramcontent.com/pod-product-compliance
Lightning Source LLC
Chambersburg PA
CBHW051726170526
45167CB00002B/816